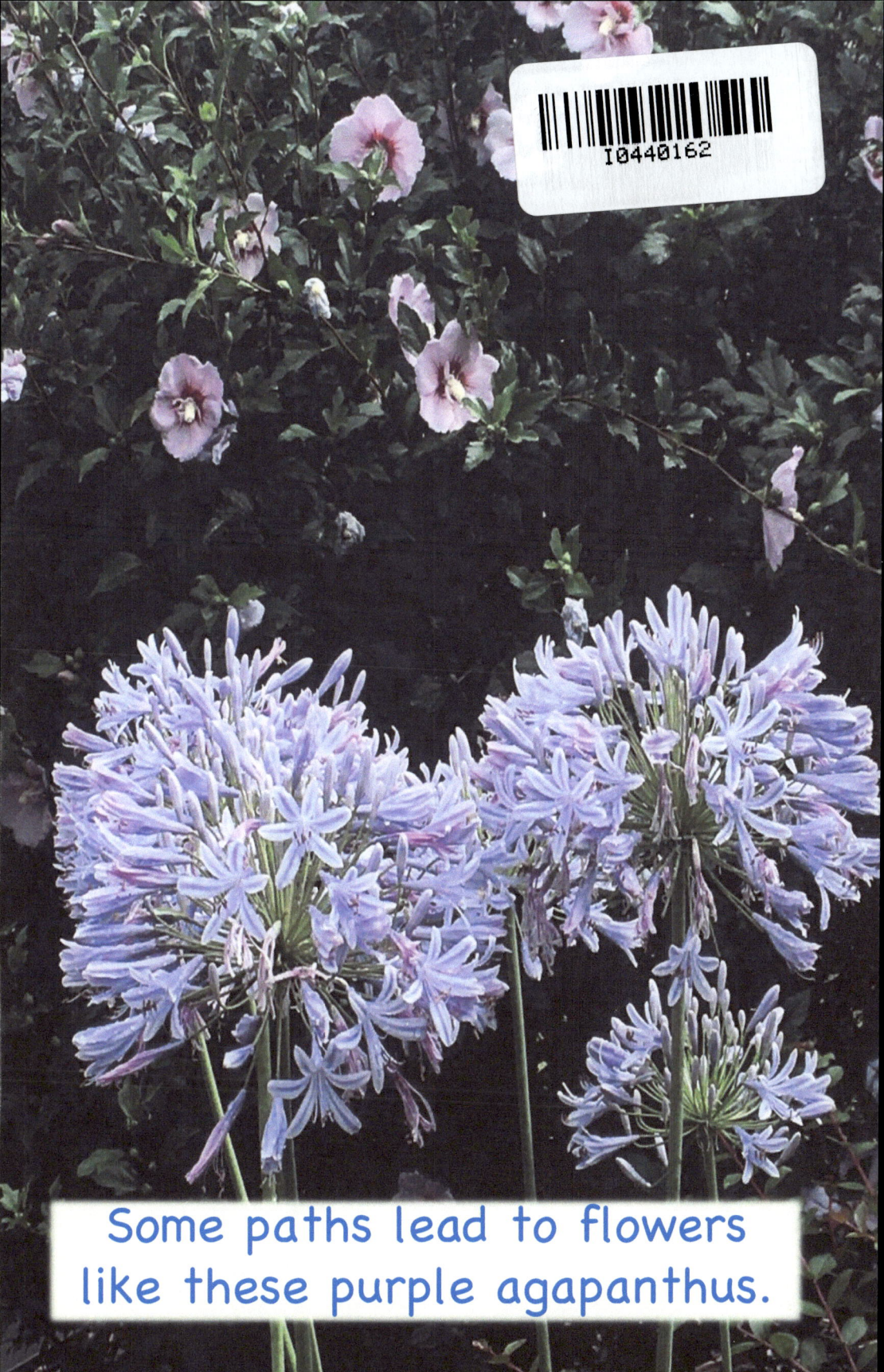

Some paths lead to flowers like these purple agapanthus.

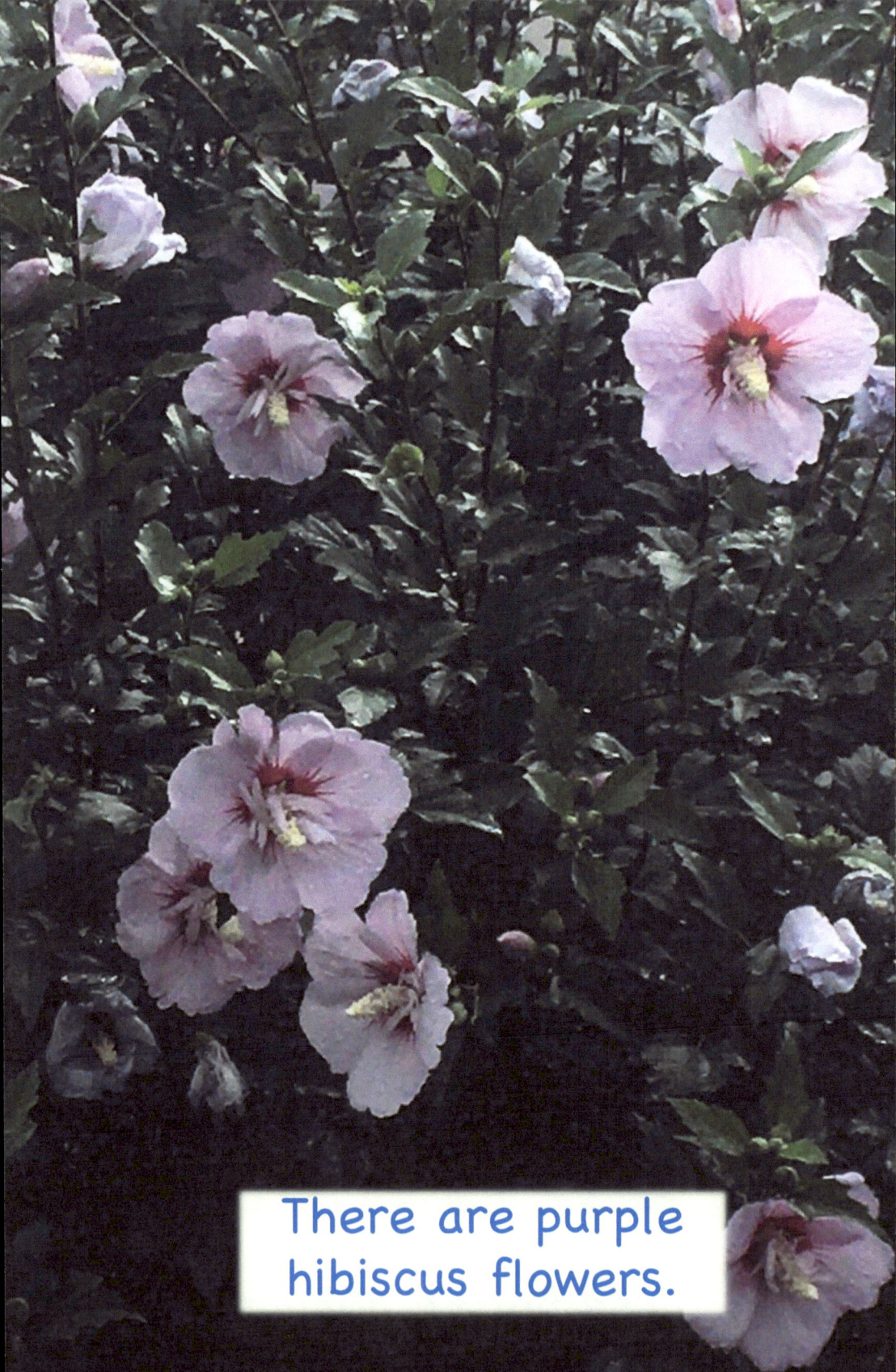

There are purple
hibiscus flowers.

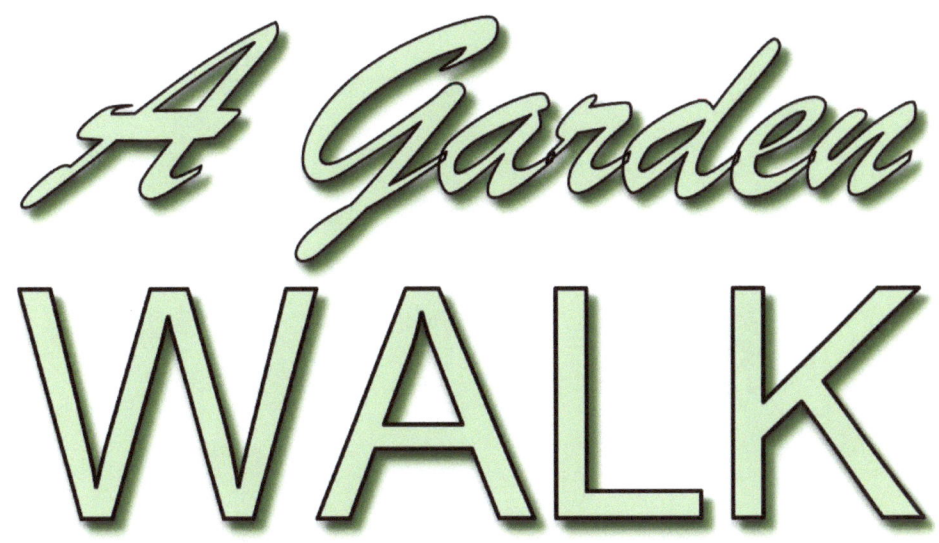

PICTURE BOOK

Mister E Press

Photos and text by Peter Evans.

NO A.I.

If you enjoyed reading this book, please consider adding a review to Amazon.

ISBN-13: 9798866566983

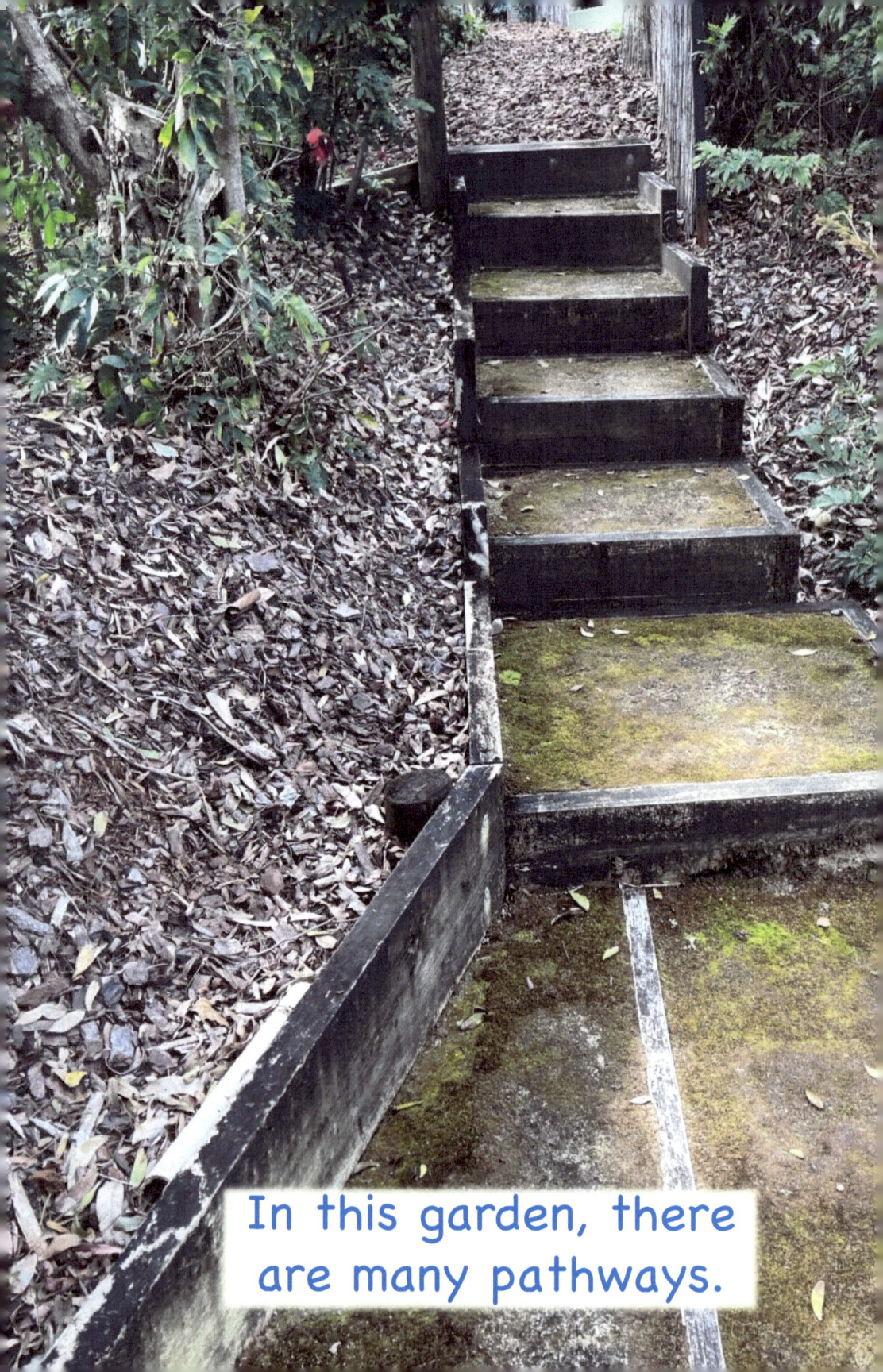

In this garden, there are many pathways.

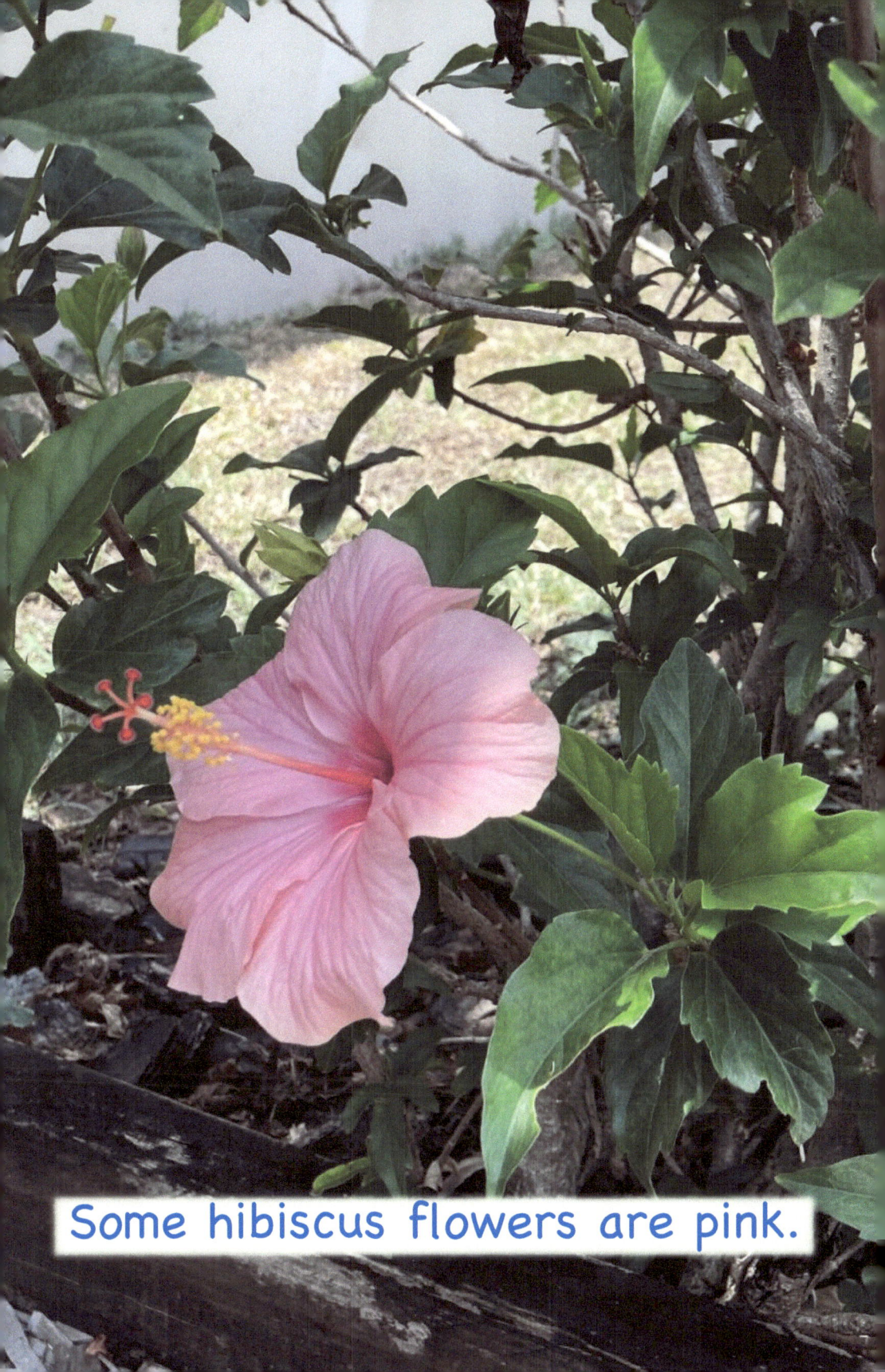

Some hibiscus flowers are pink.

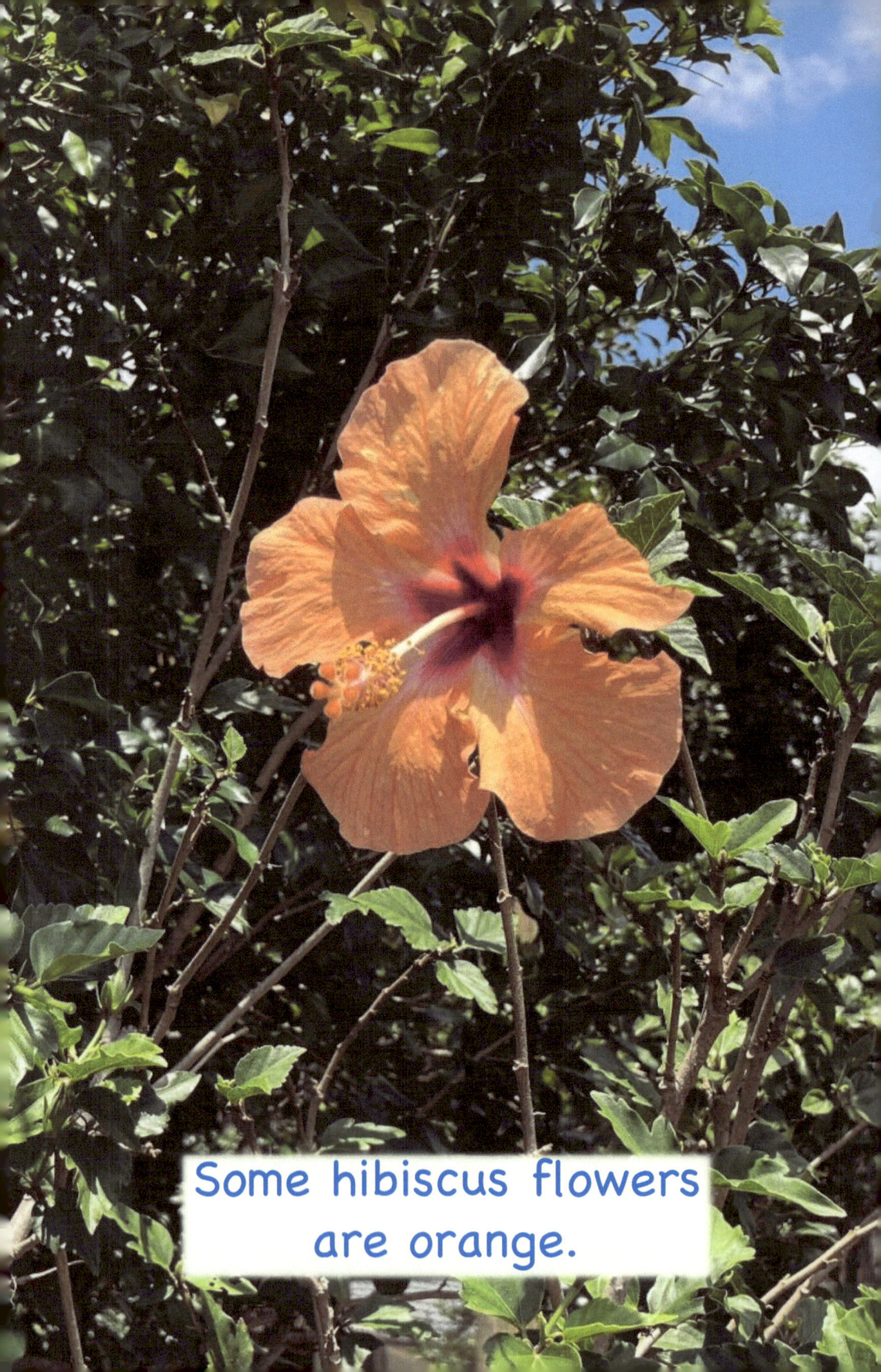

Some hibiscus flowers are orange.

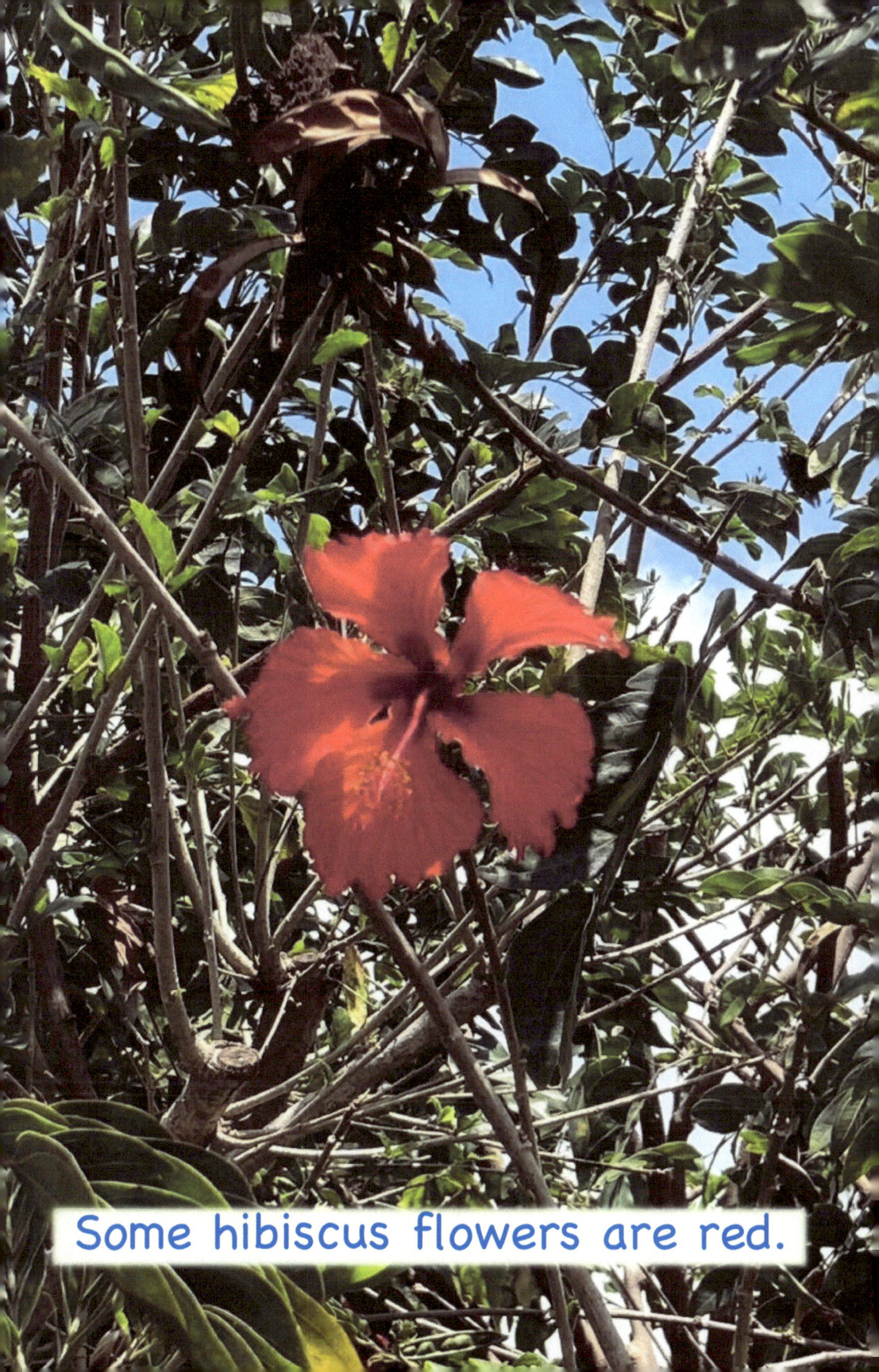

Some hibiscus flowers are red.

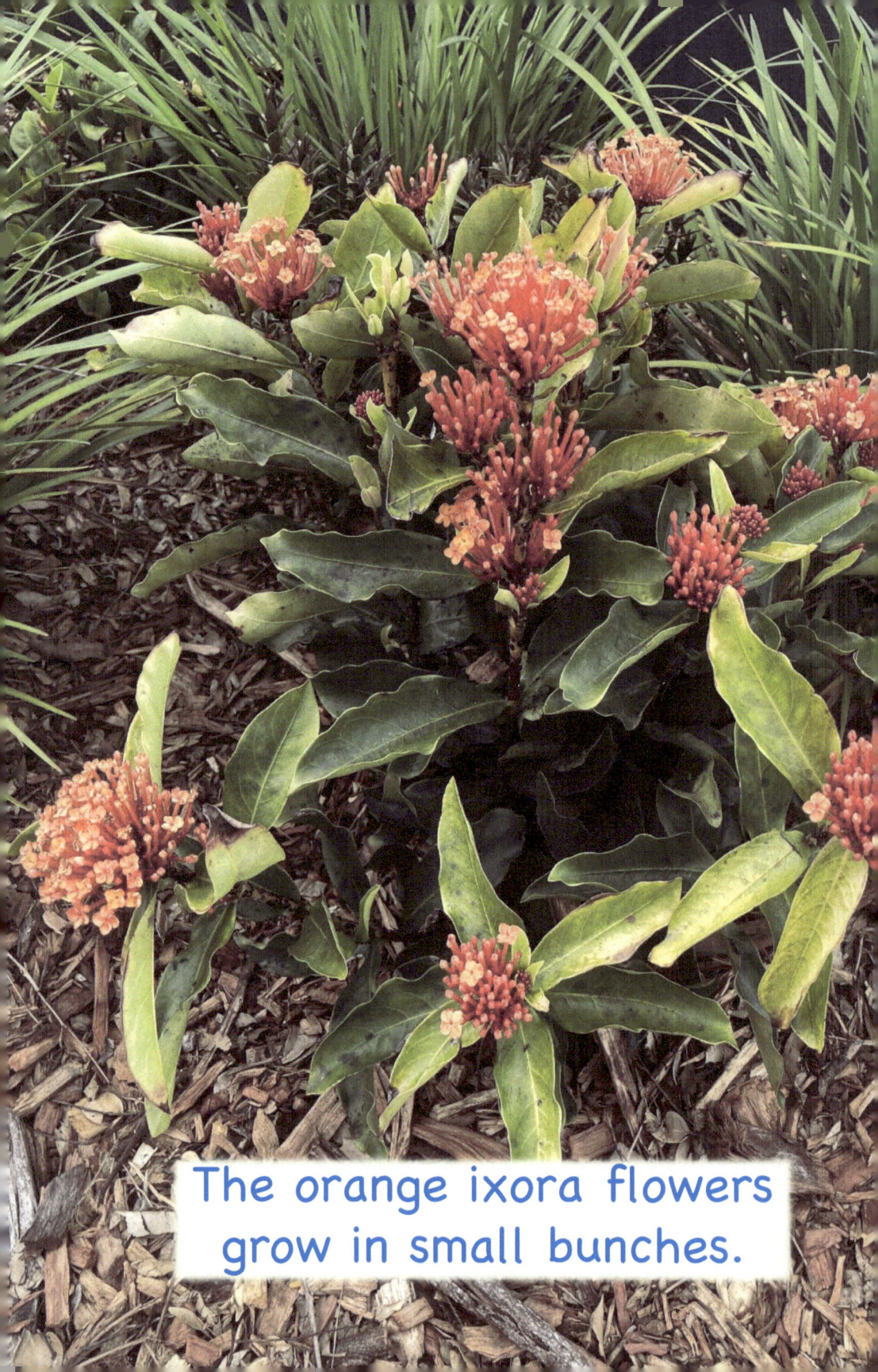

The orange ixora flowers grow in small bunches.

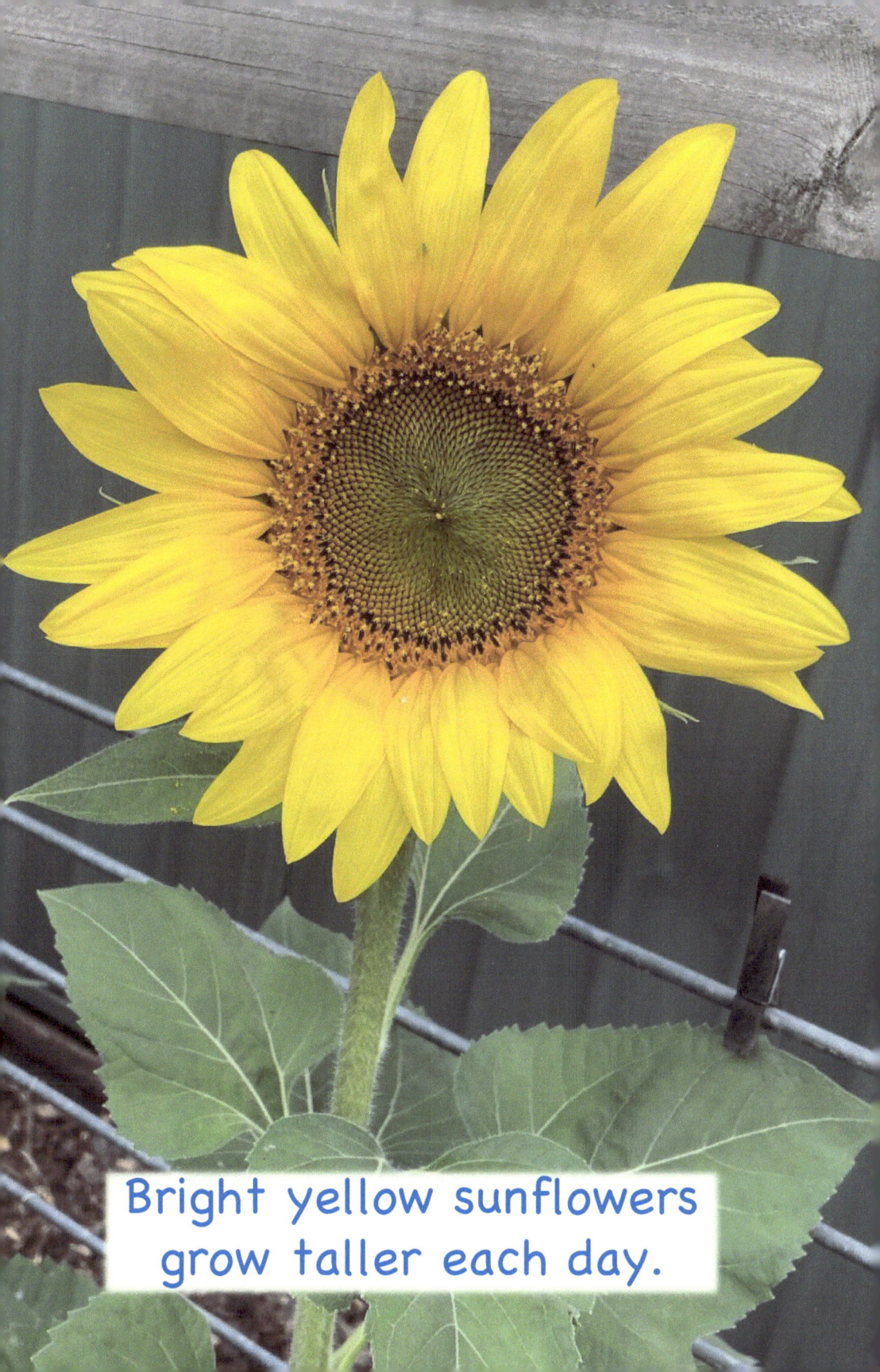

Bright yellow sunflowers
grow taller each day.

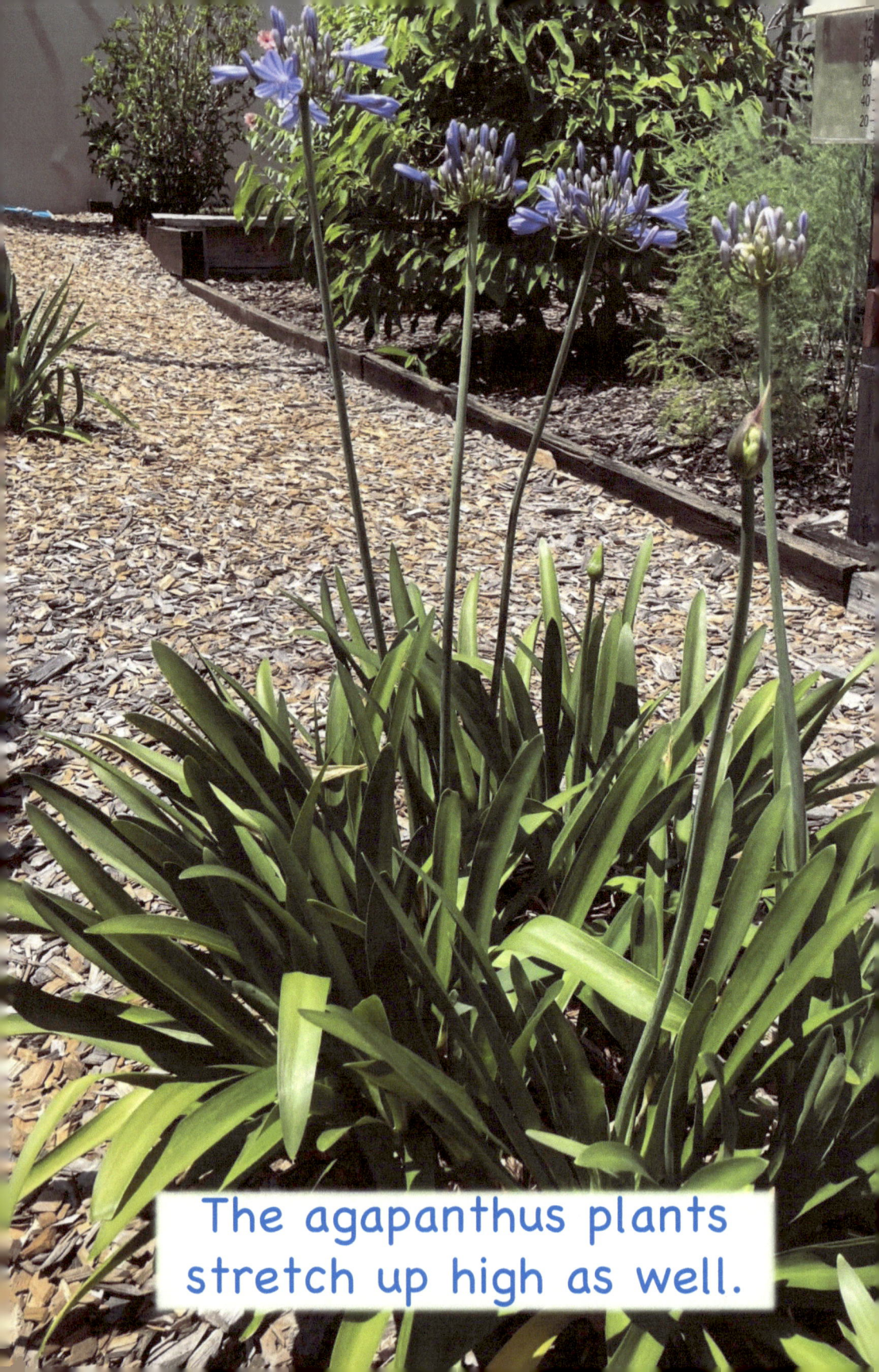

The agapanthus plants stretch up high as well.

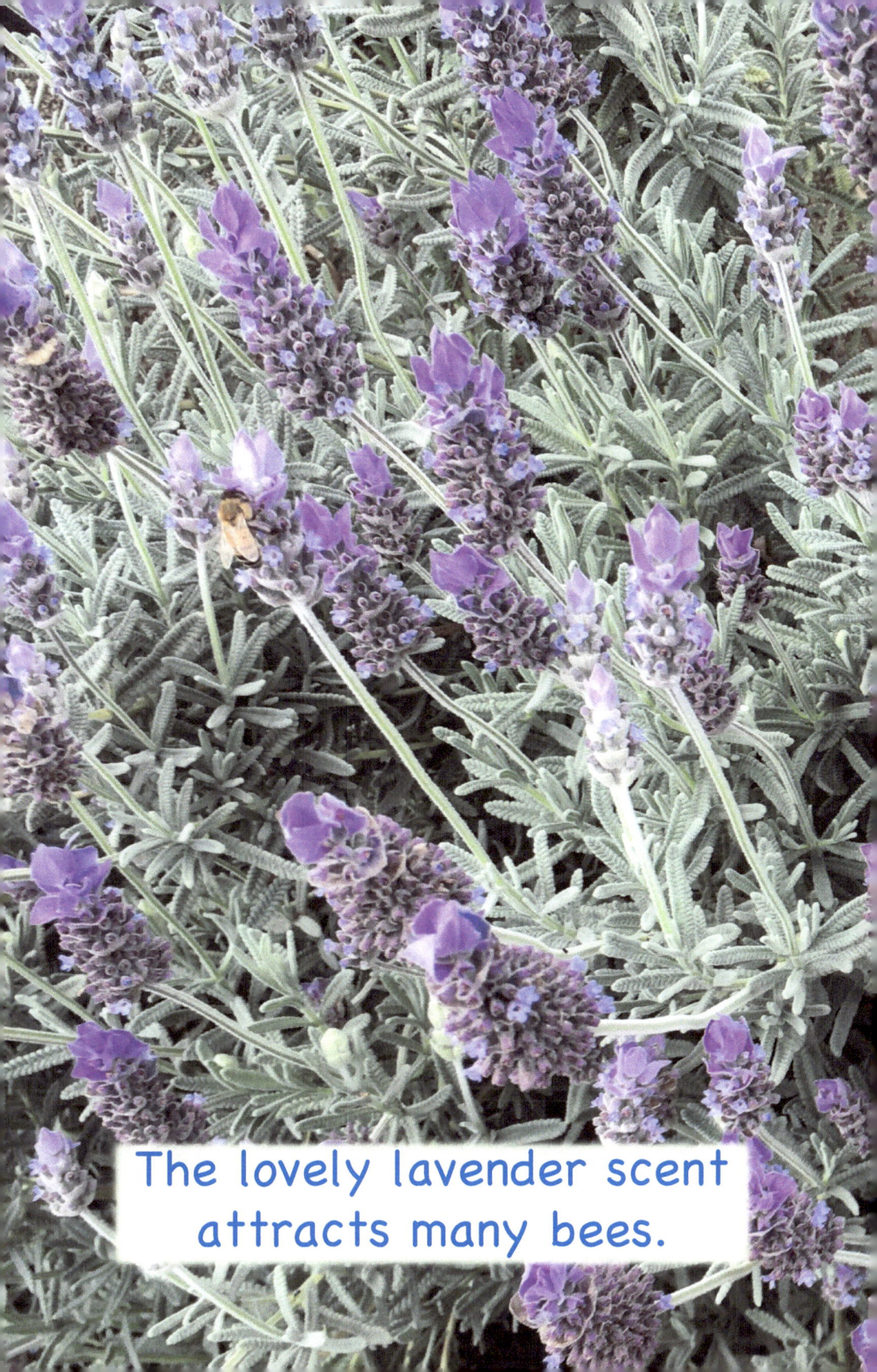

The lovely lavender scent attracts many bees.

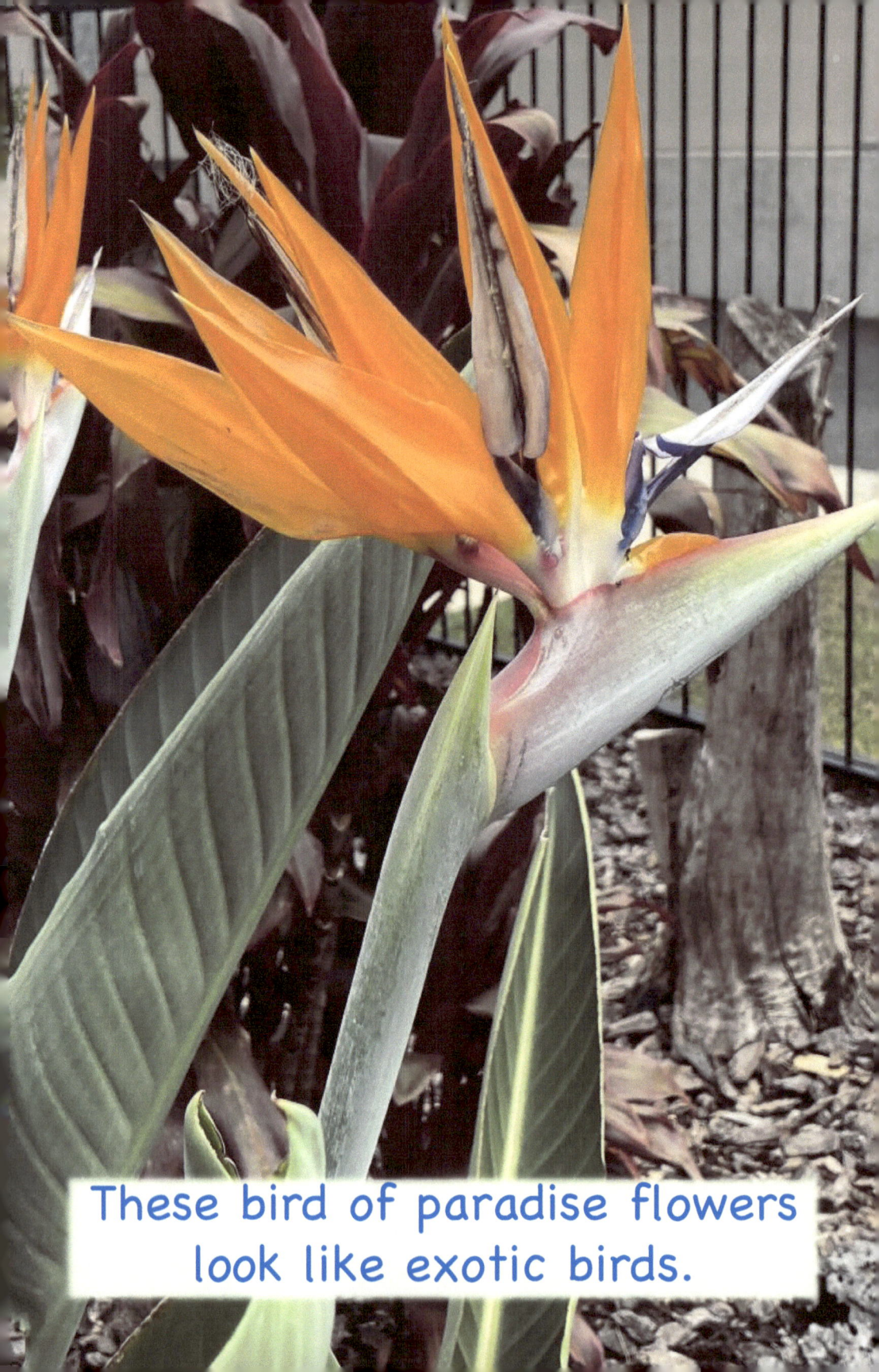

These bird of paradise flowers look like exotic birds.

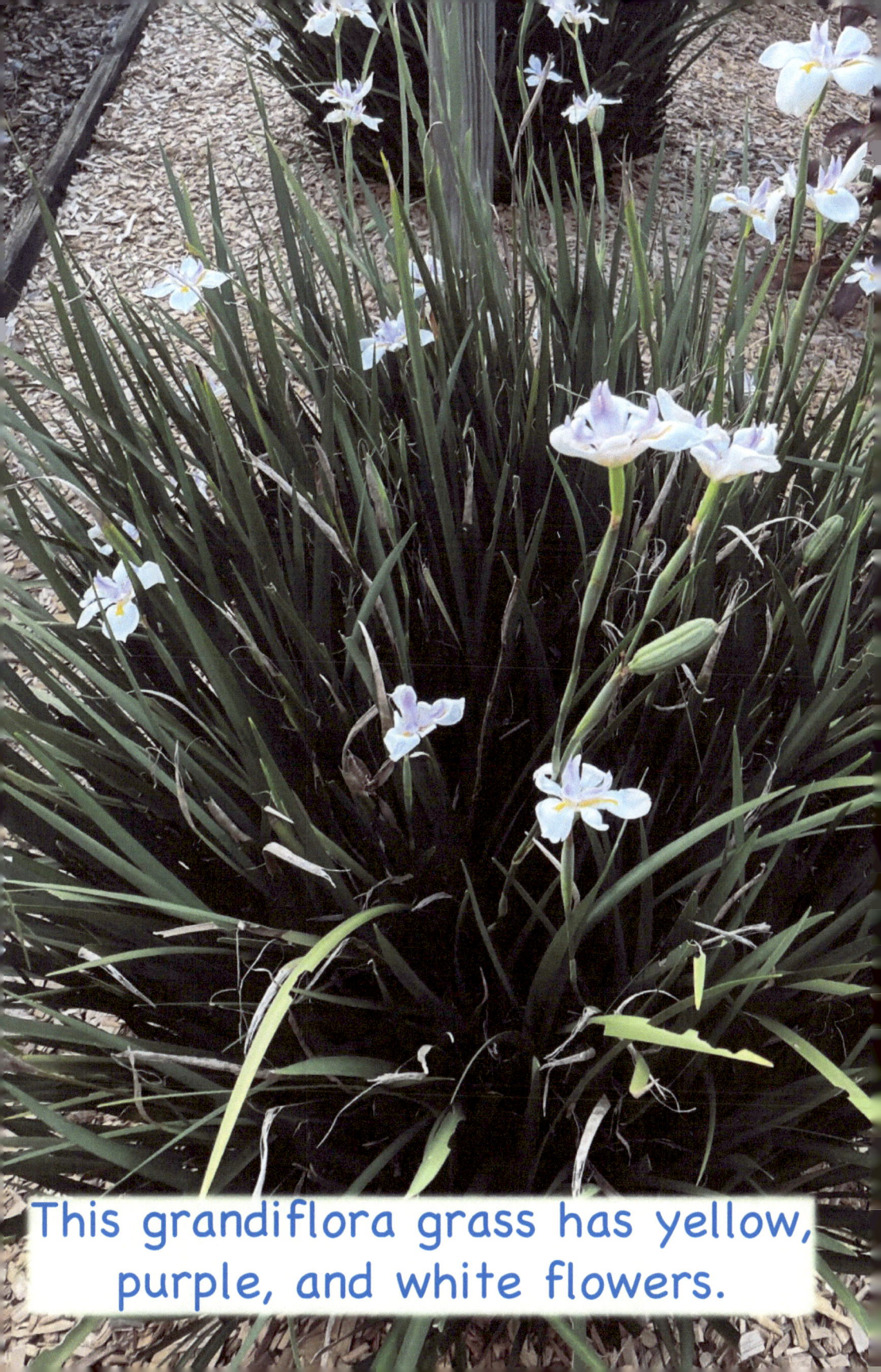

This grandiflora grass has yellow, purple, and white flowers.

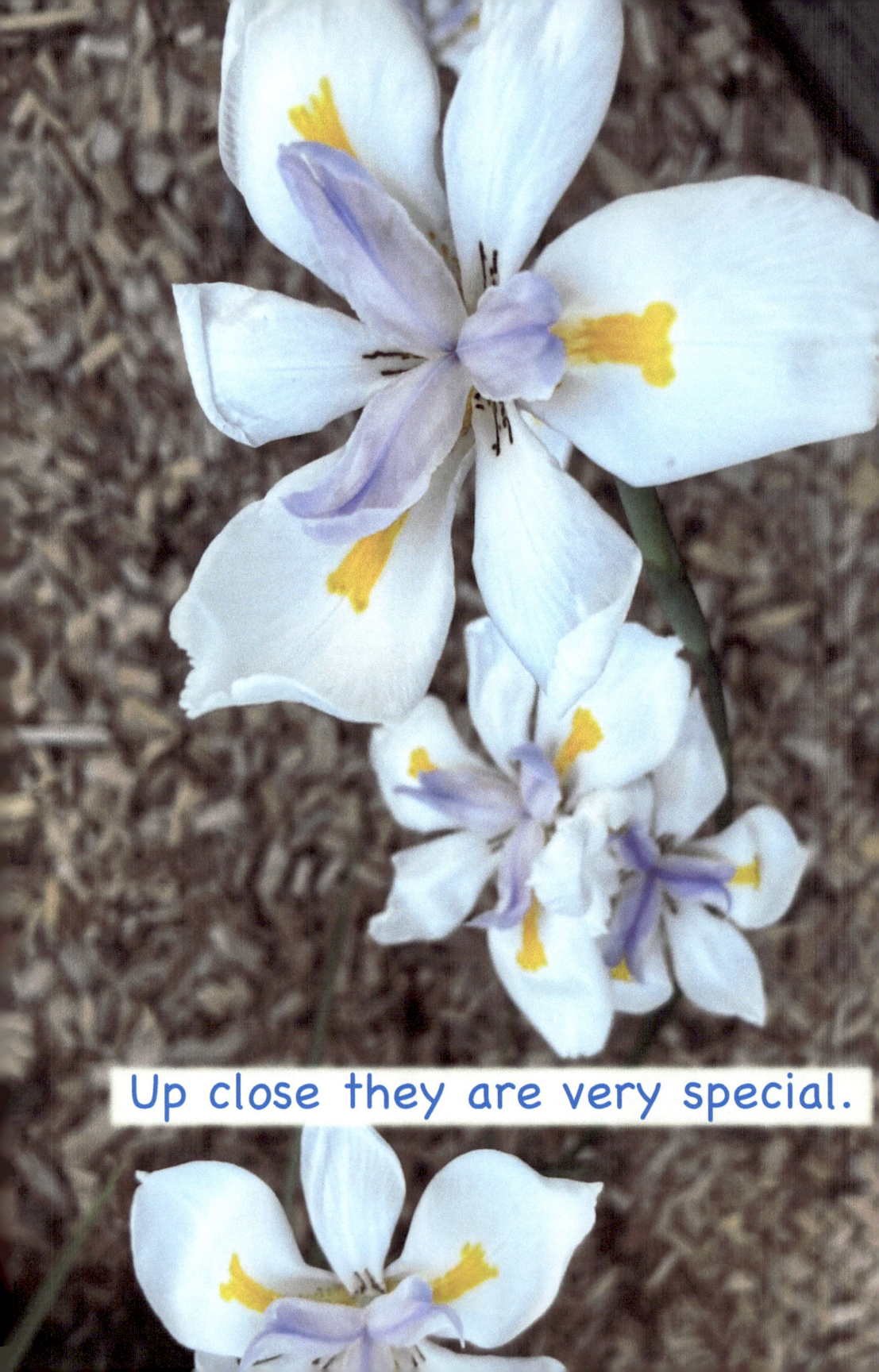

Up close they are very special.

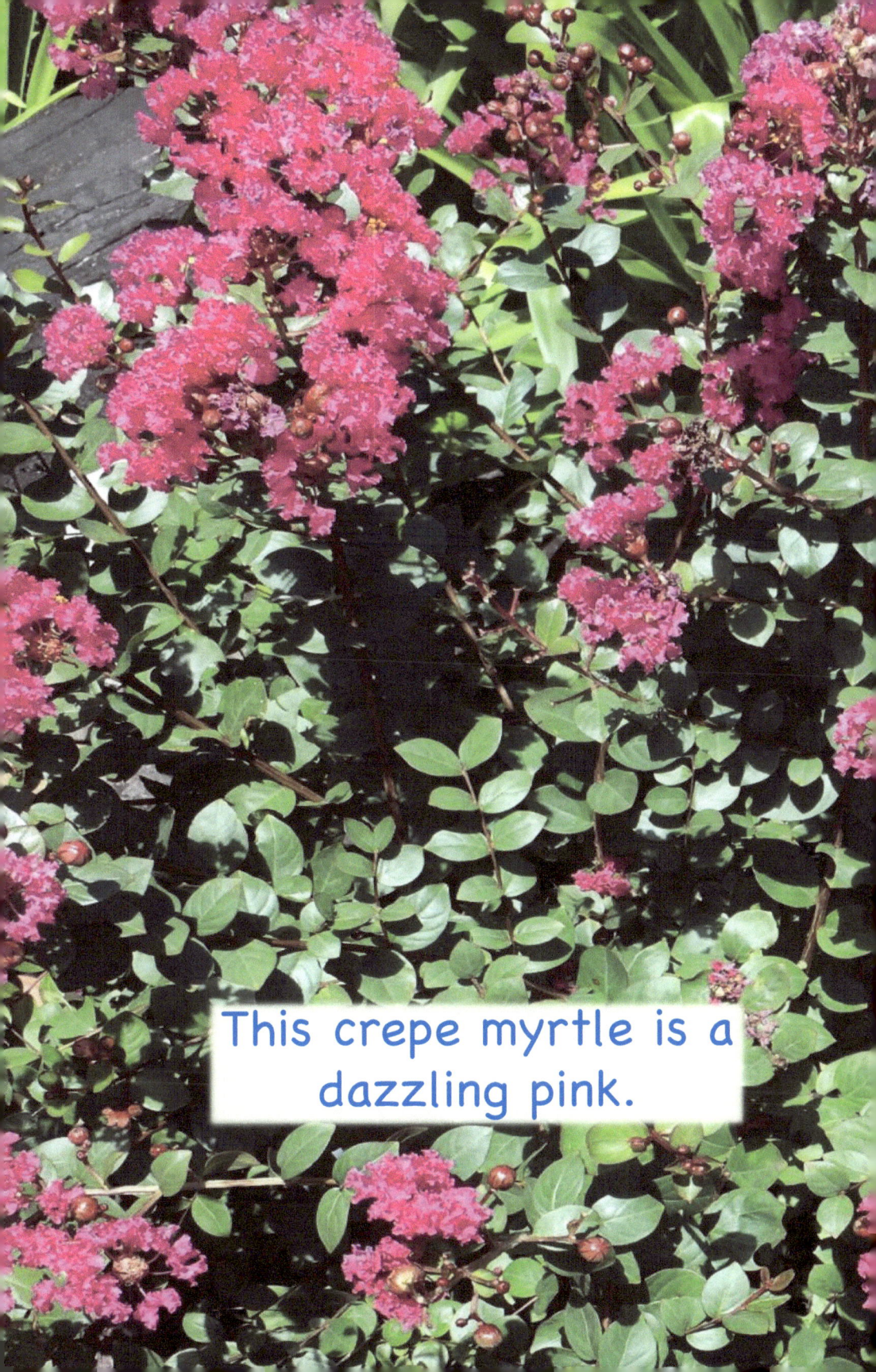

This crepe myrtle is a dazzling pink.

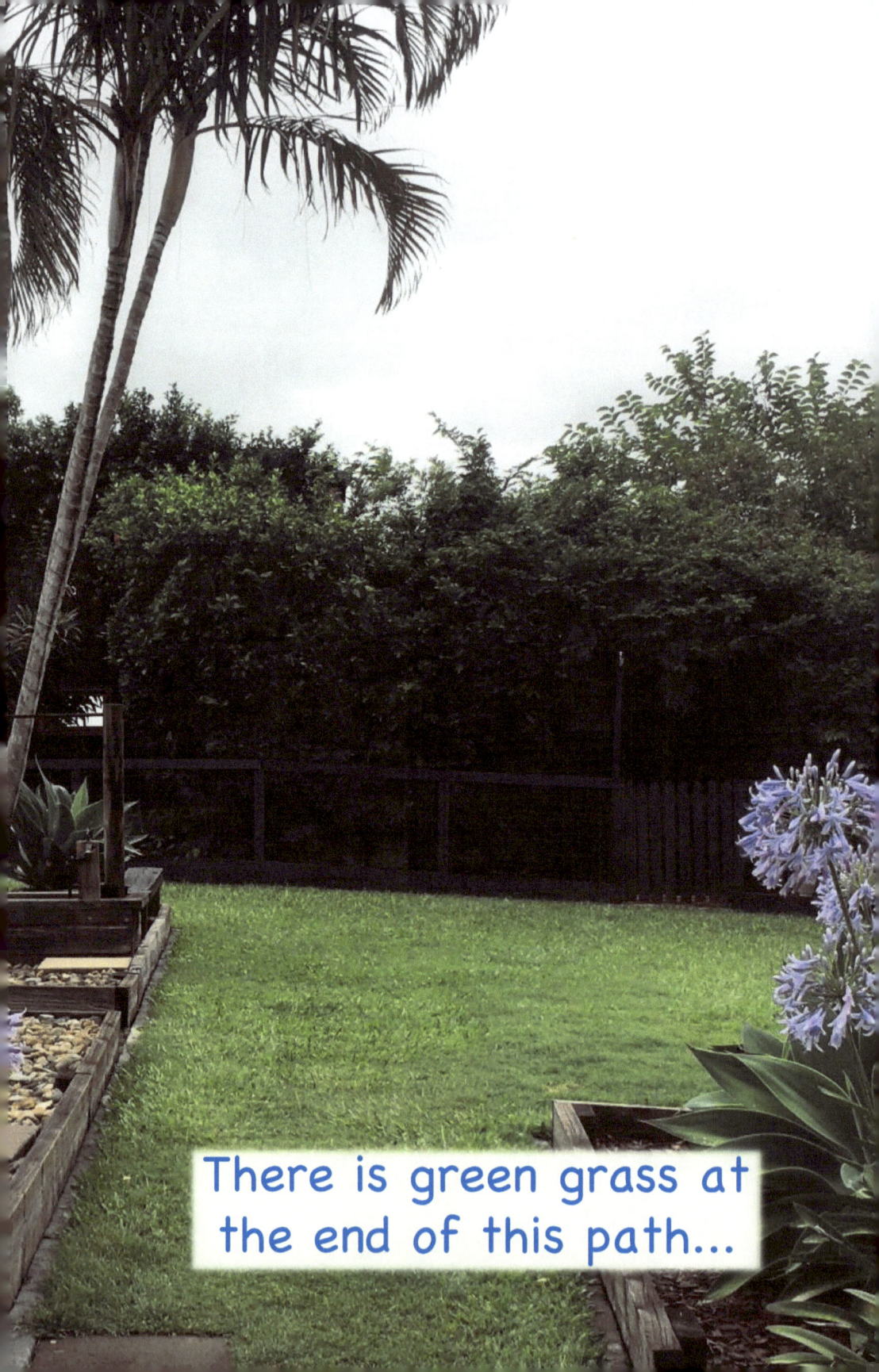

There is green grass at
the end of this path...

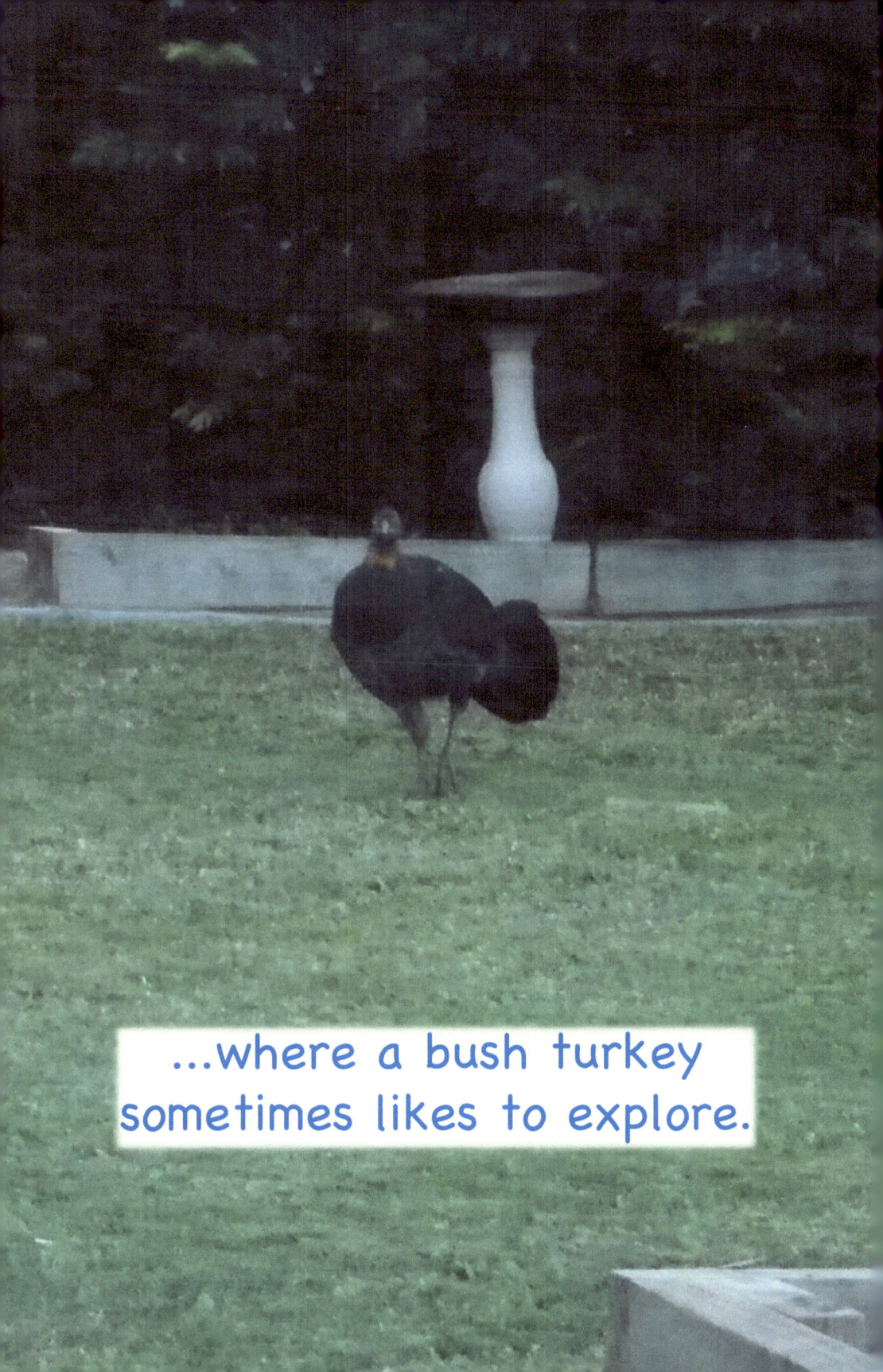

...where a bush turkey
sometimes likes to explore.

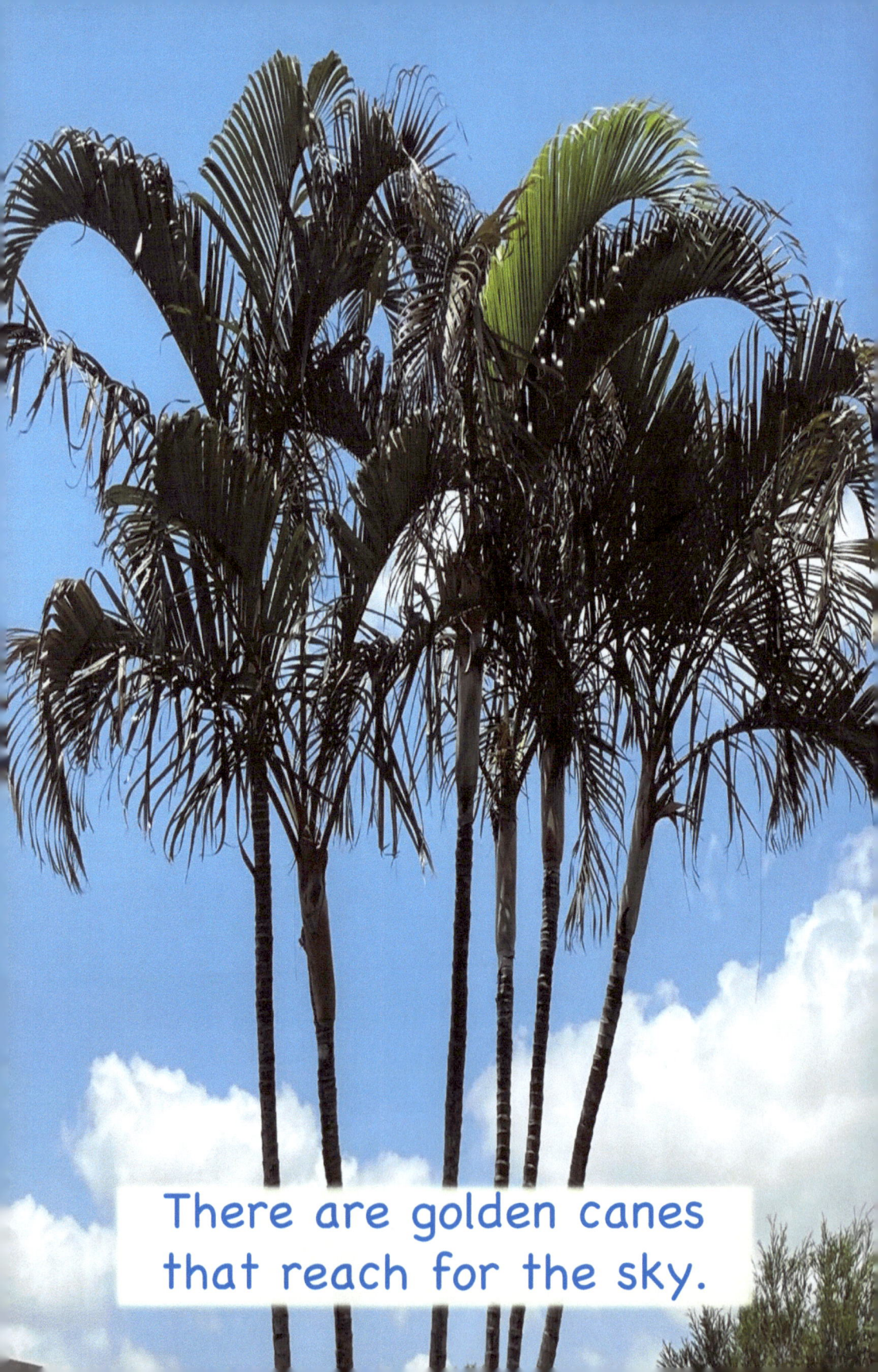

There are golden canes
that reach for the sky.

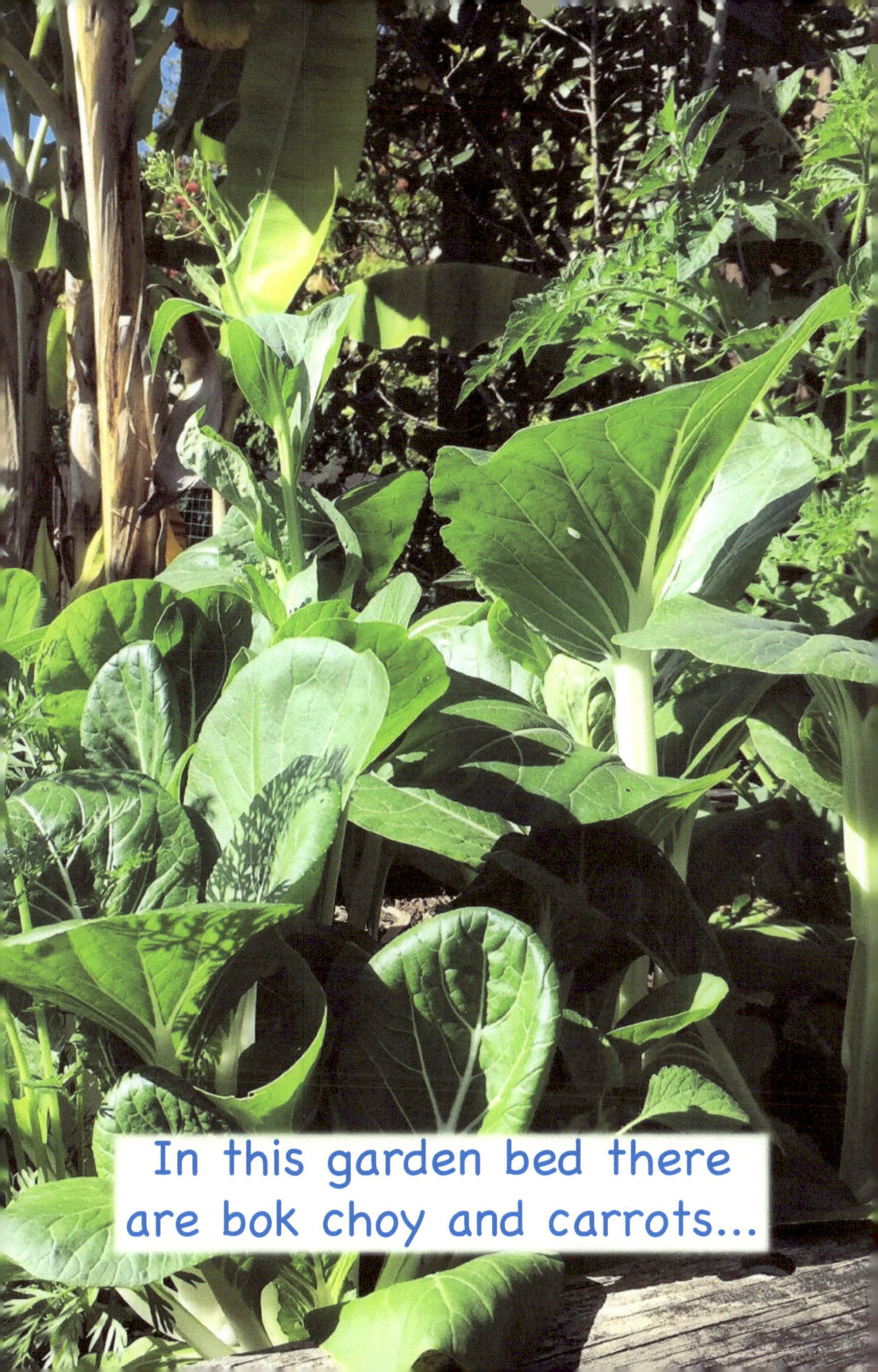

In this garden bed there are bok choy and carrots...

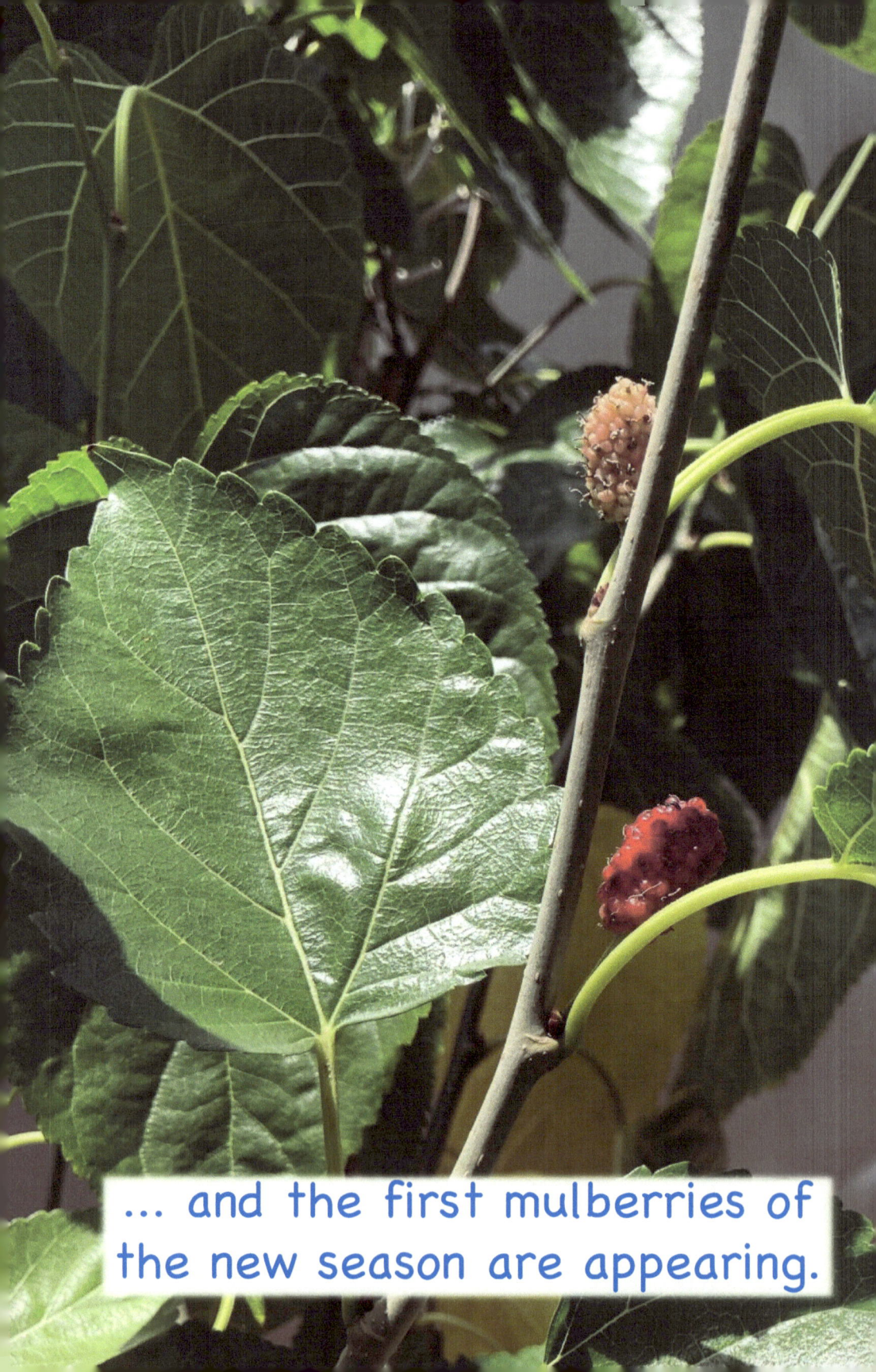

... and the first mulberries of the new season are appearing.

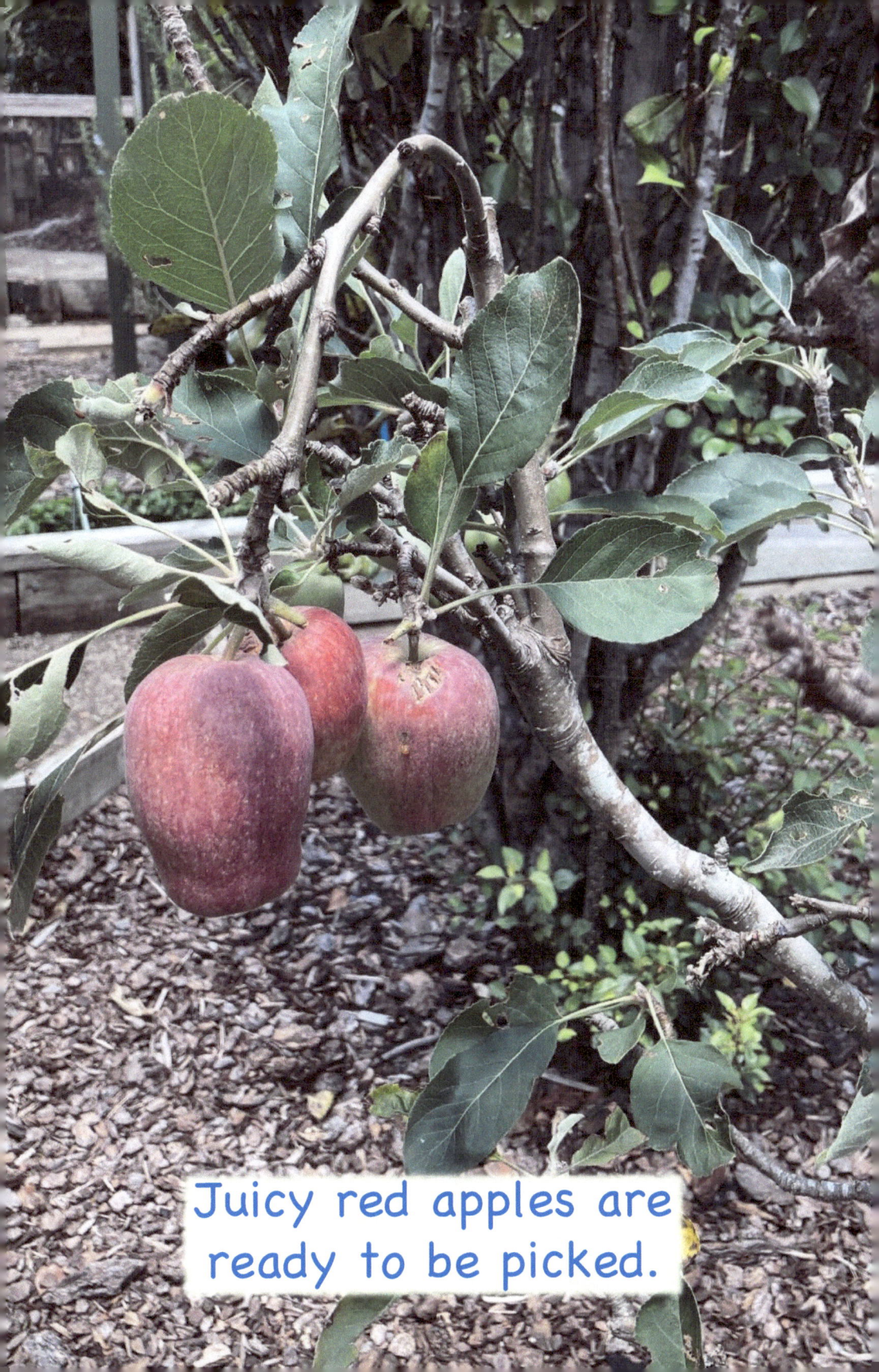

Juicy red apples are ready to be picked.

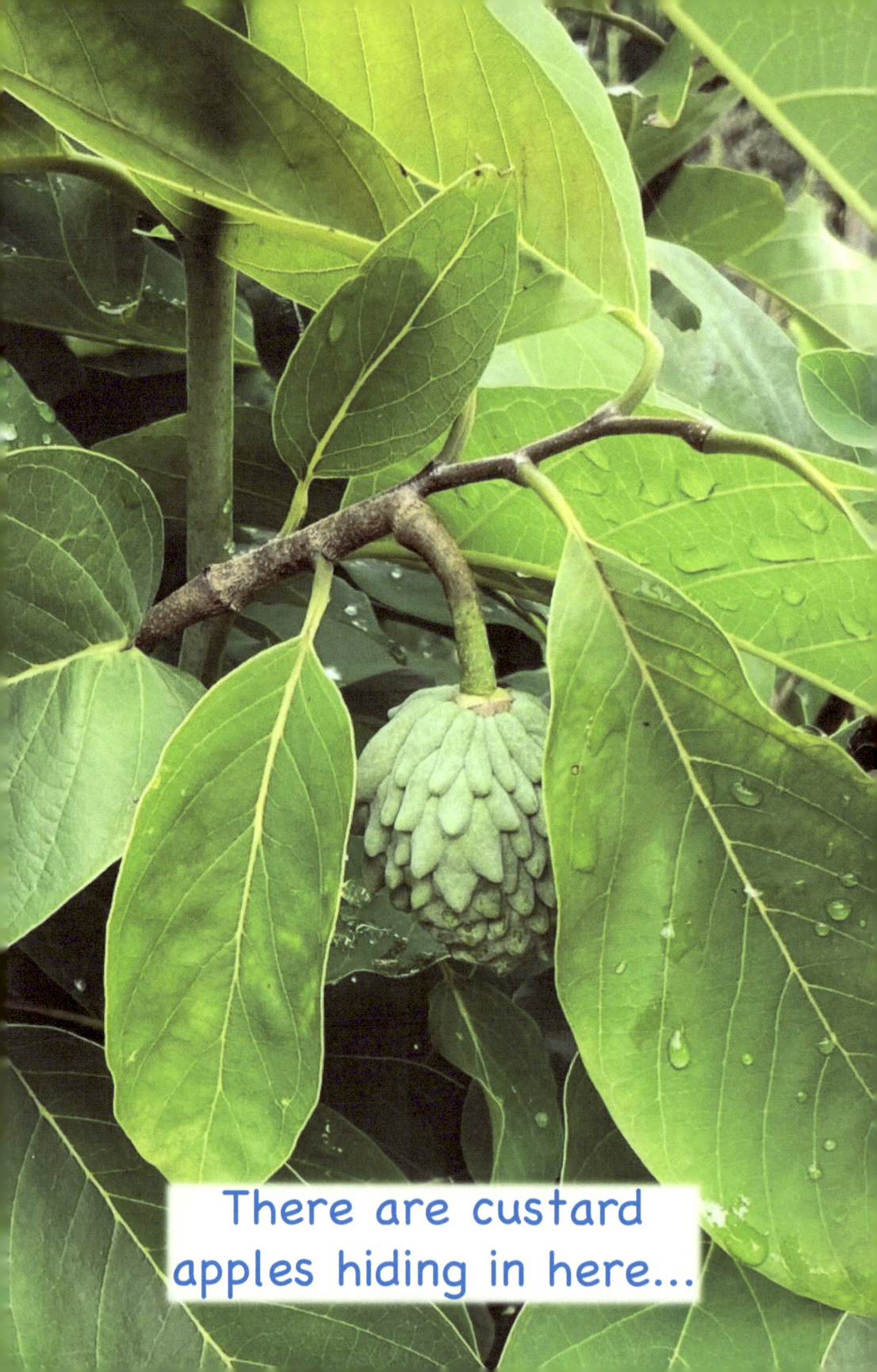

There are custard
apples hiding in here...

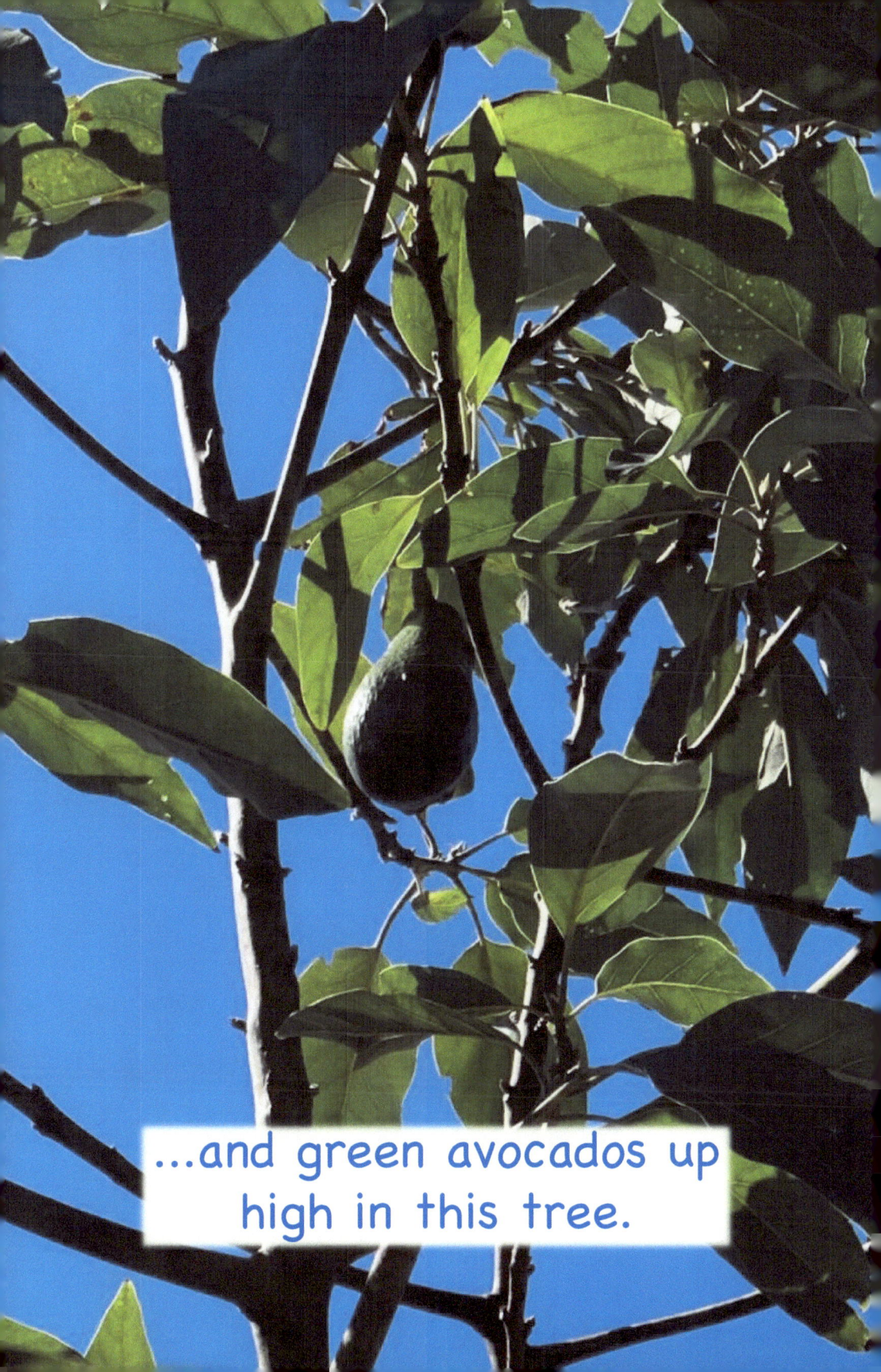

...and green avocados up high in this tree.

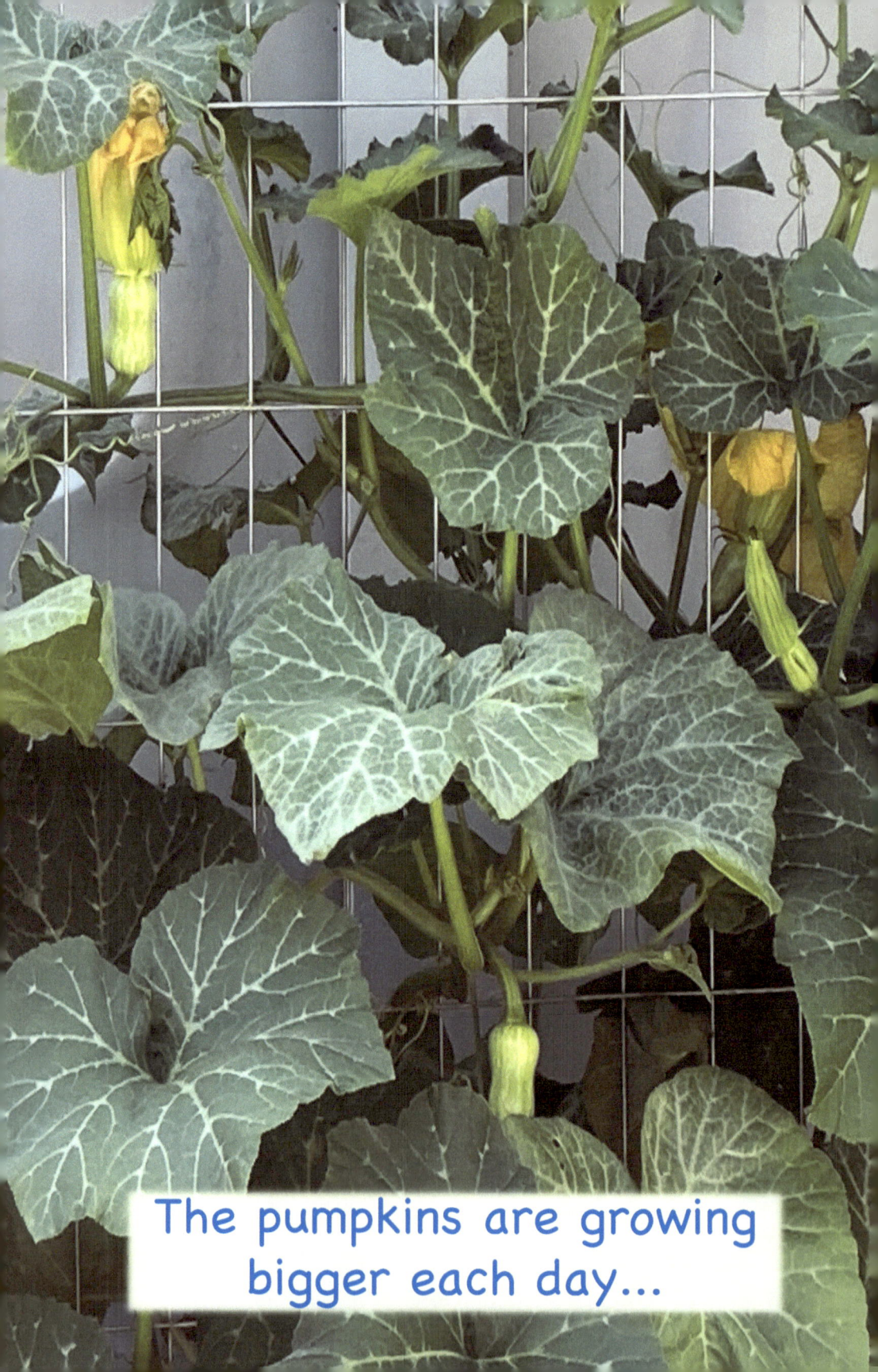

The pumpkins are growing
bigger each day...

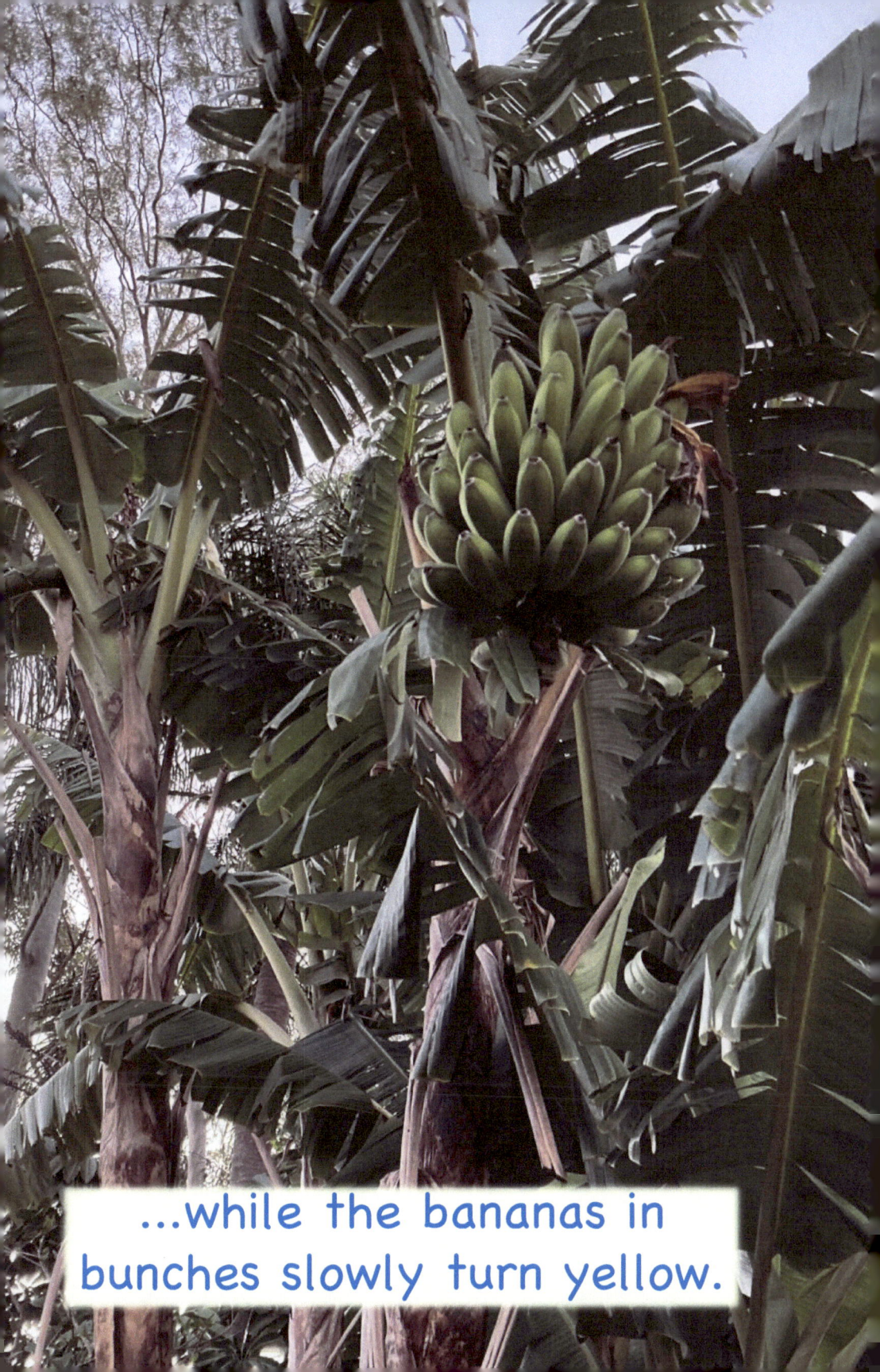

...while the bananas in bunches slowly turn yellow.

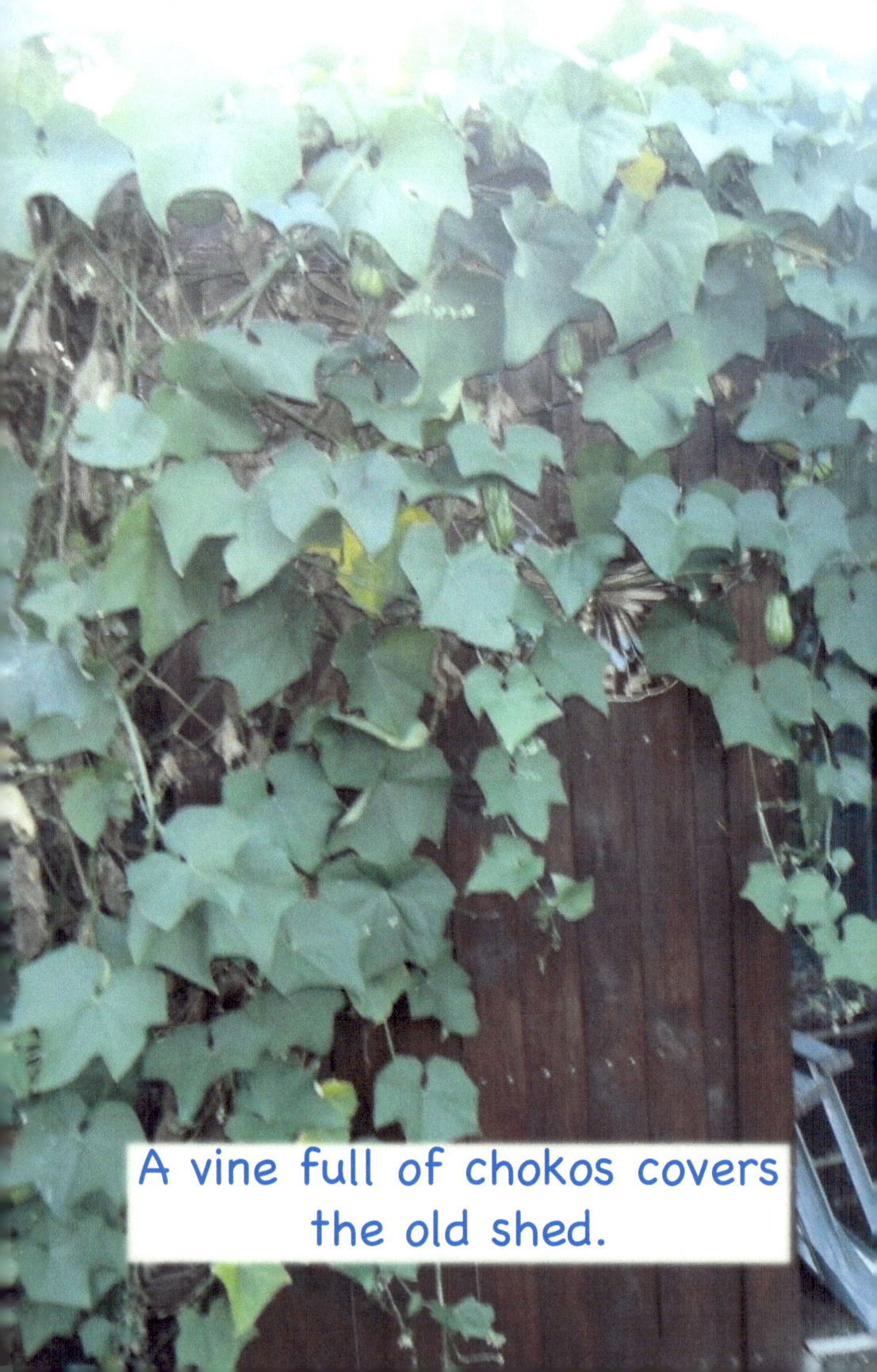

A vine full of chokos covers the old shed.

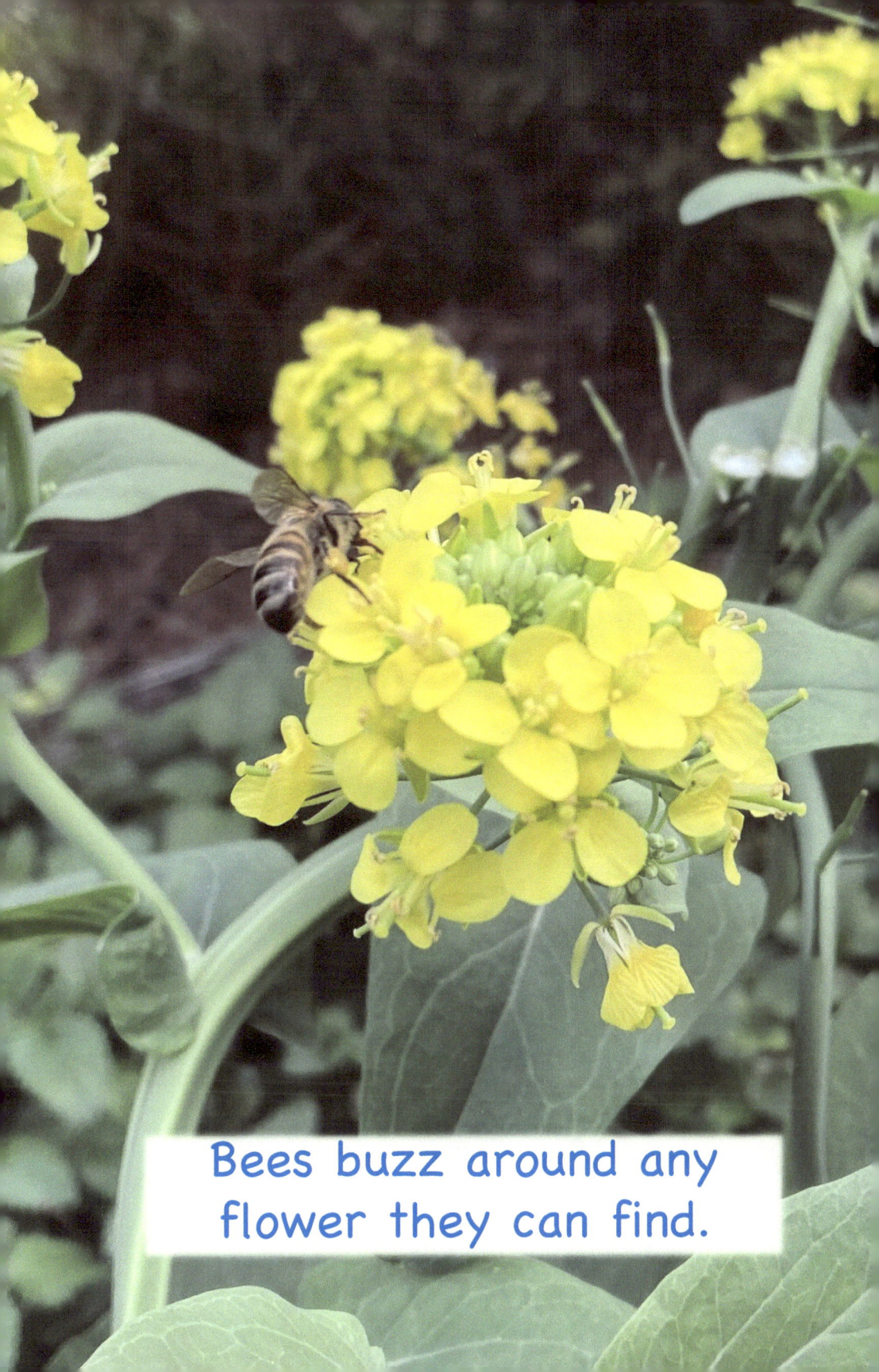

Bees buzz around any flower they can find.

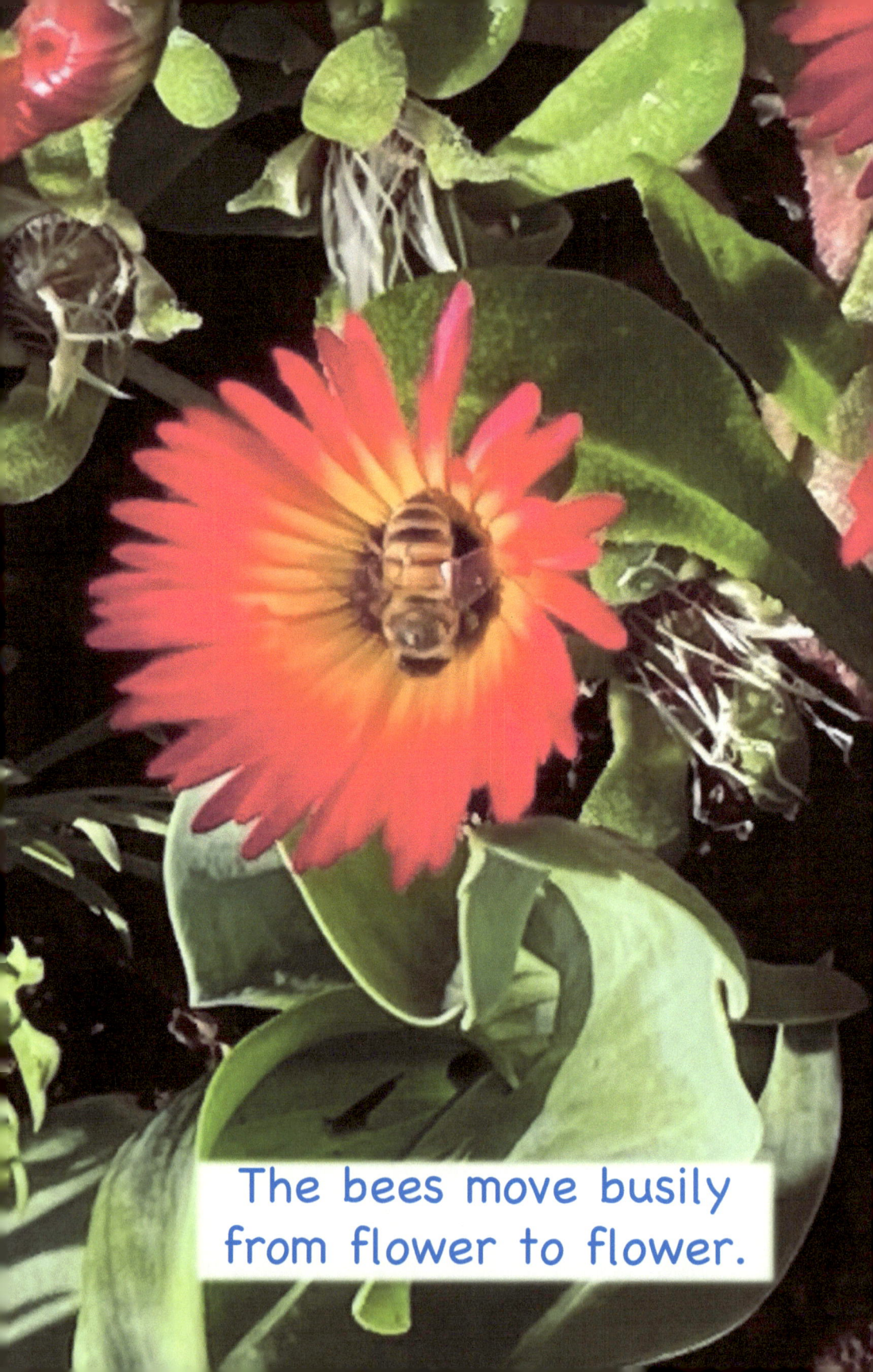

The bees move busily
from flower to flower.

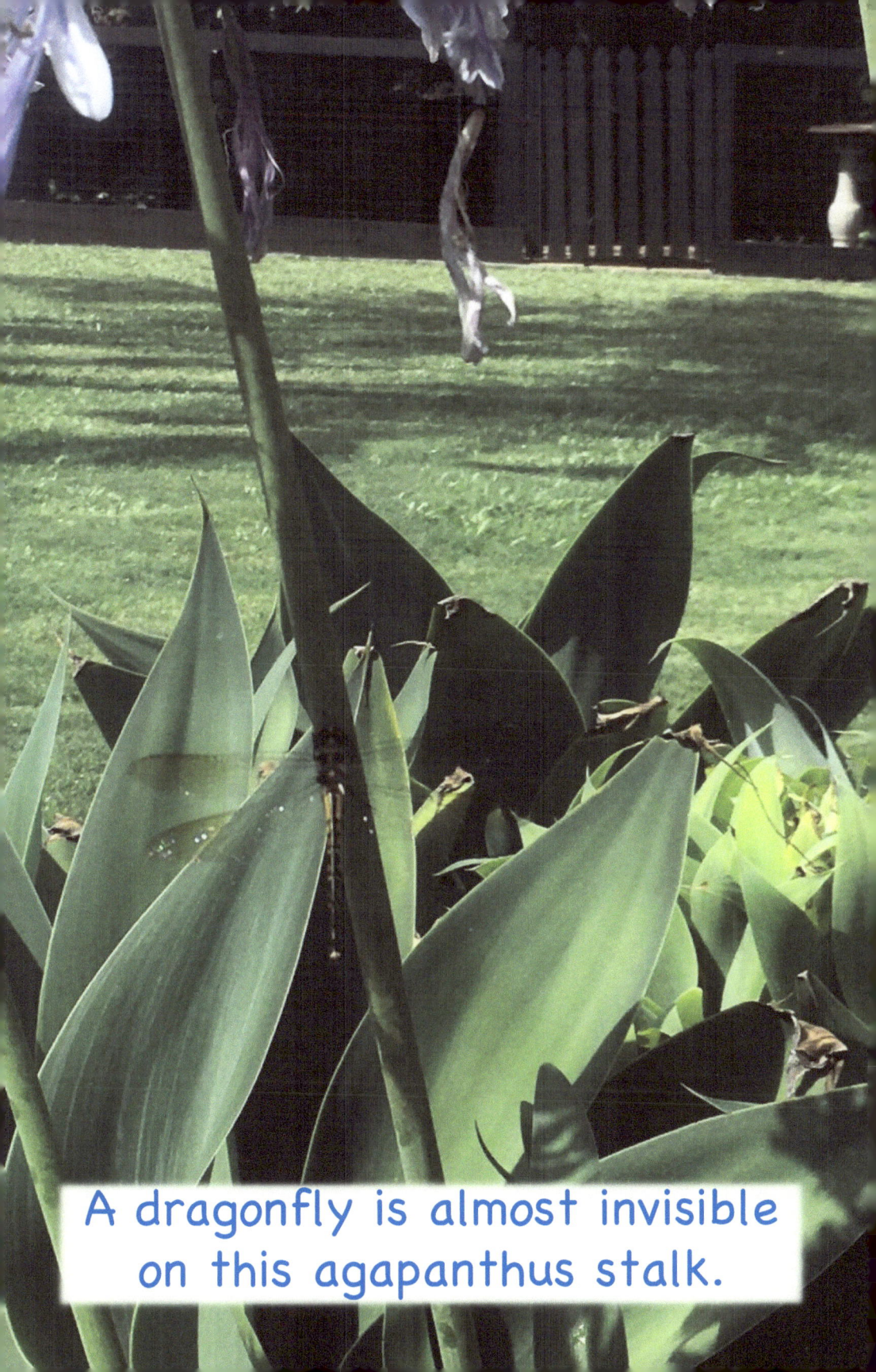

A dragonfly is almost invisible
on this agapanthus stalk.

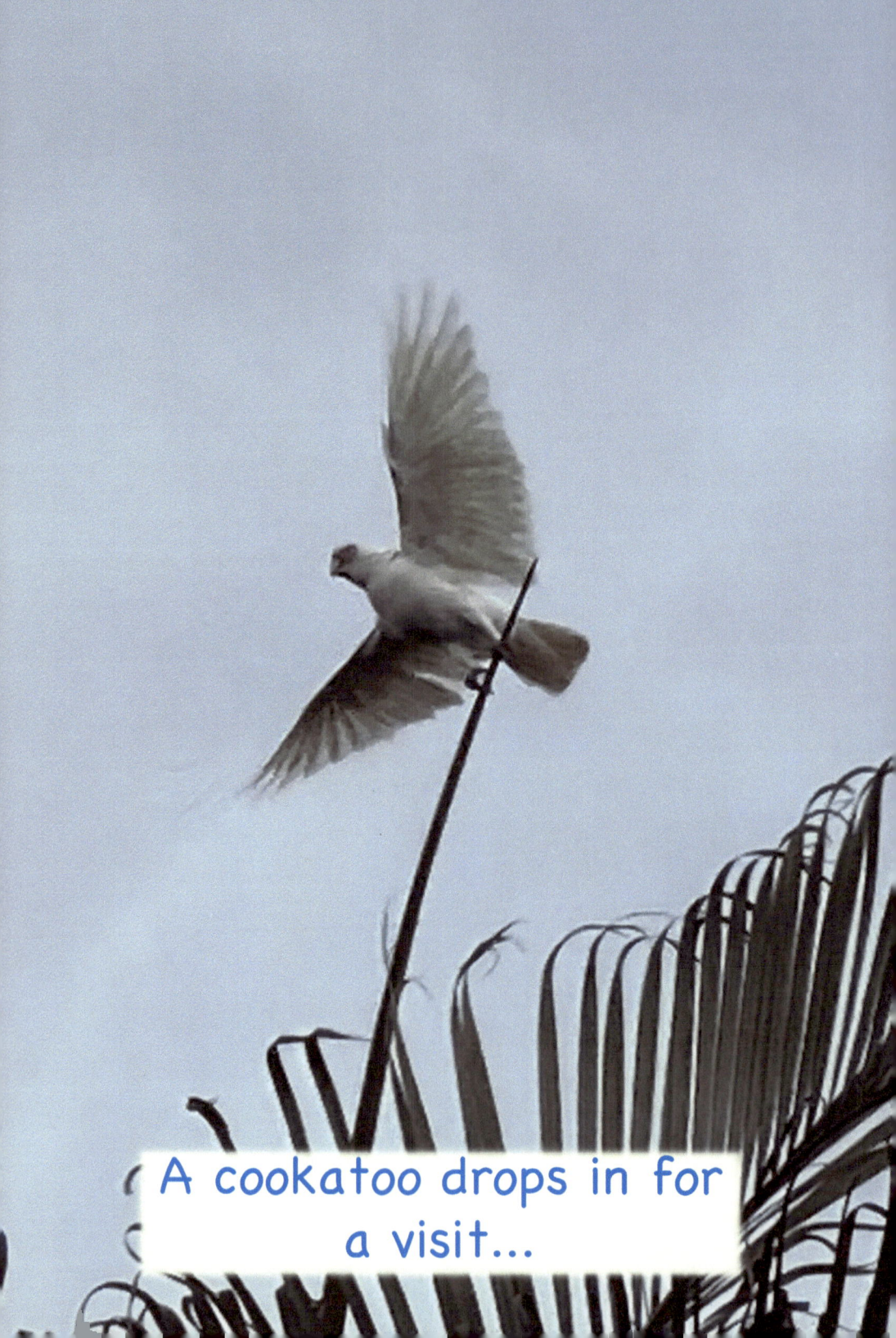

A cookatoo drops in for a visit...

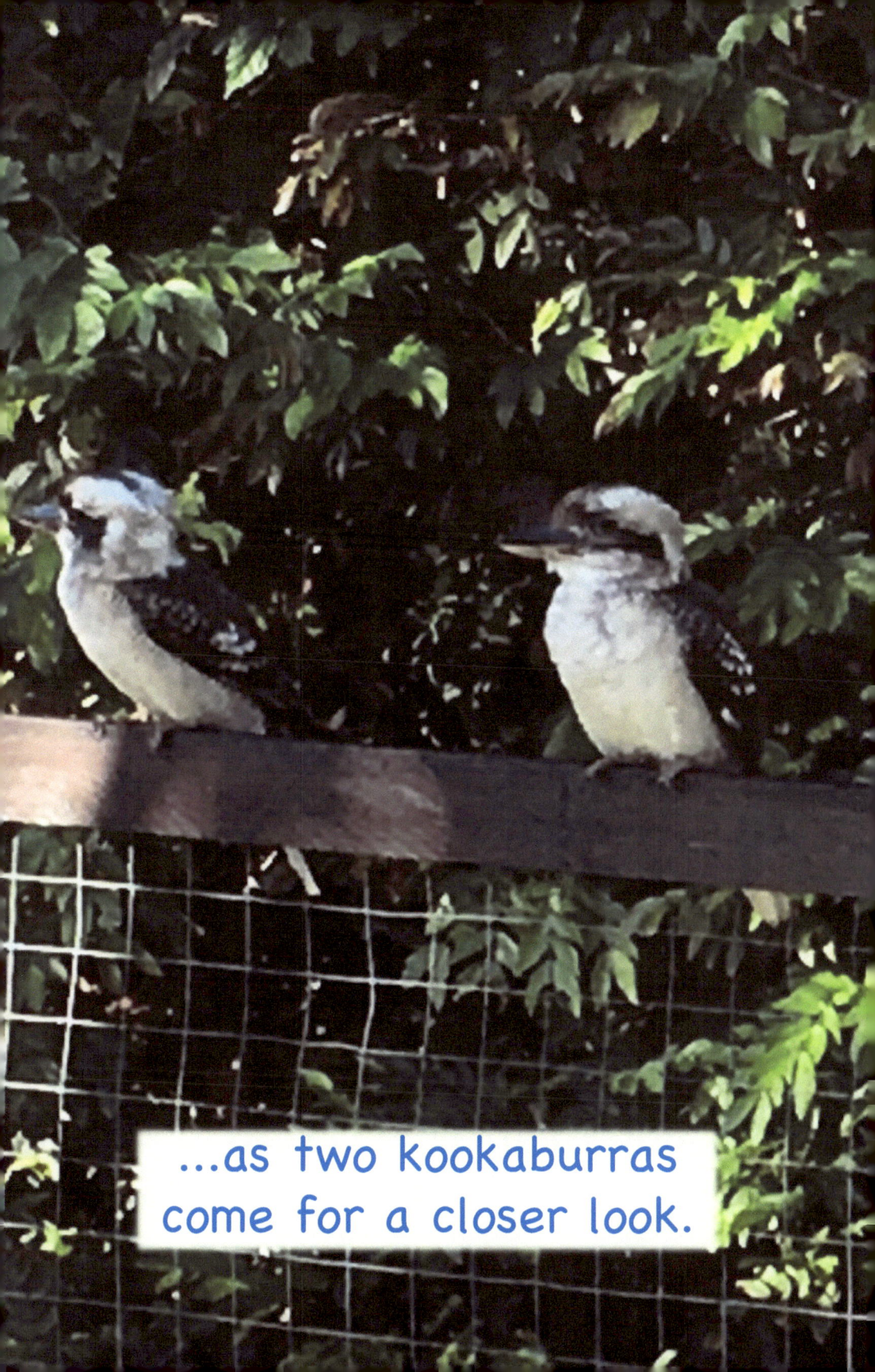

...as two kookaburras
come for a closer look.

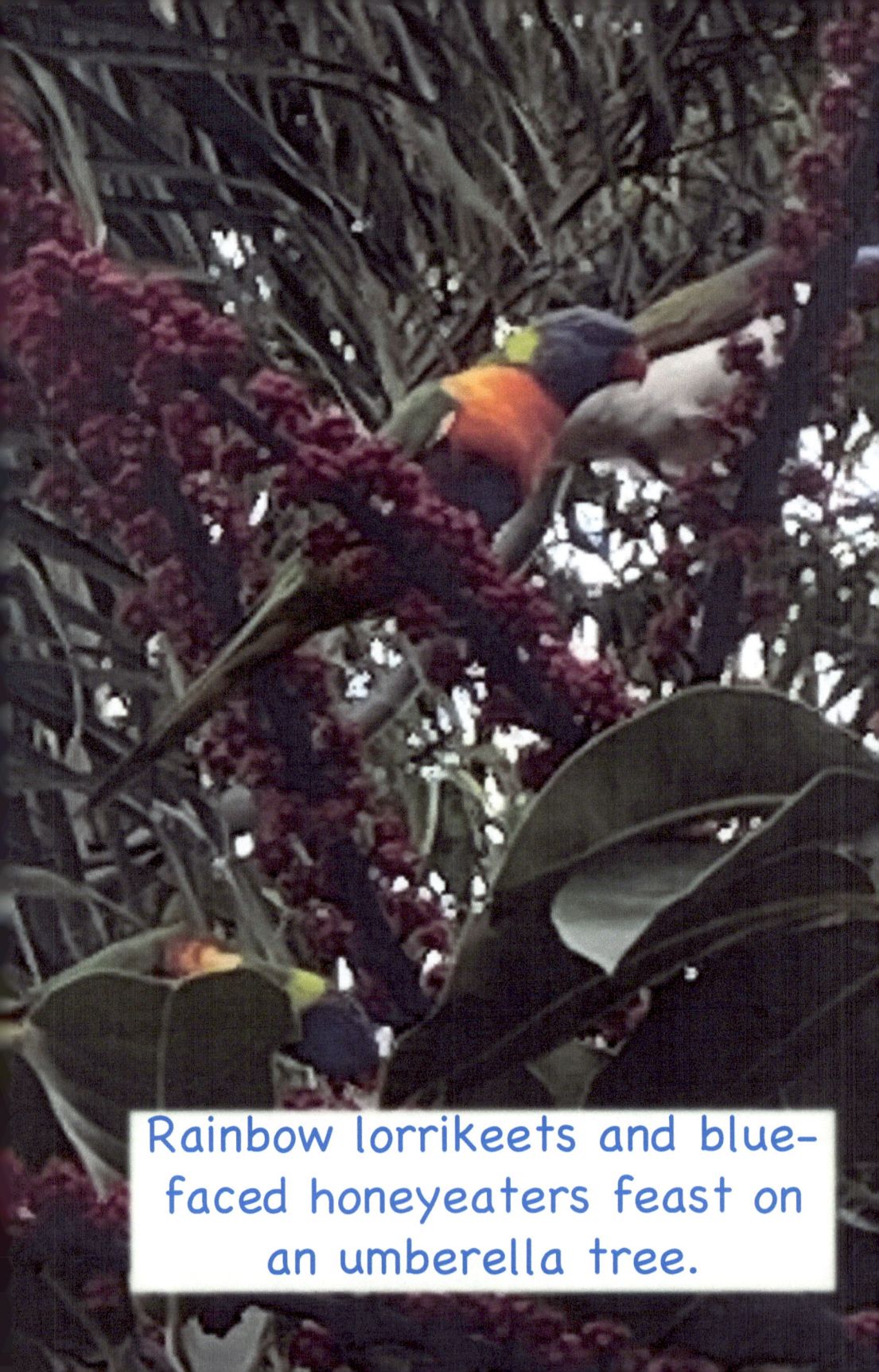

Rainbow lorrikeets and blue-faced honeyeaters feast on an umberella tree.

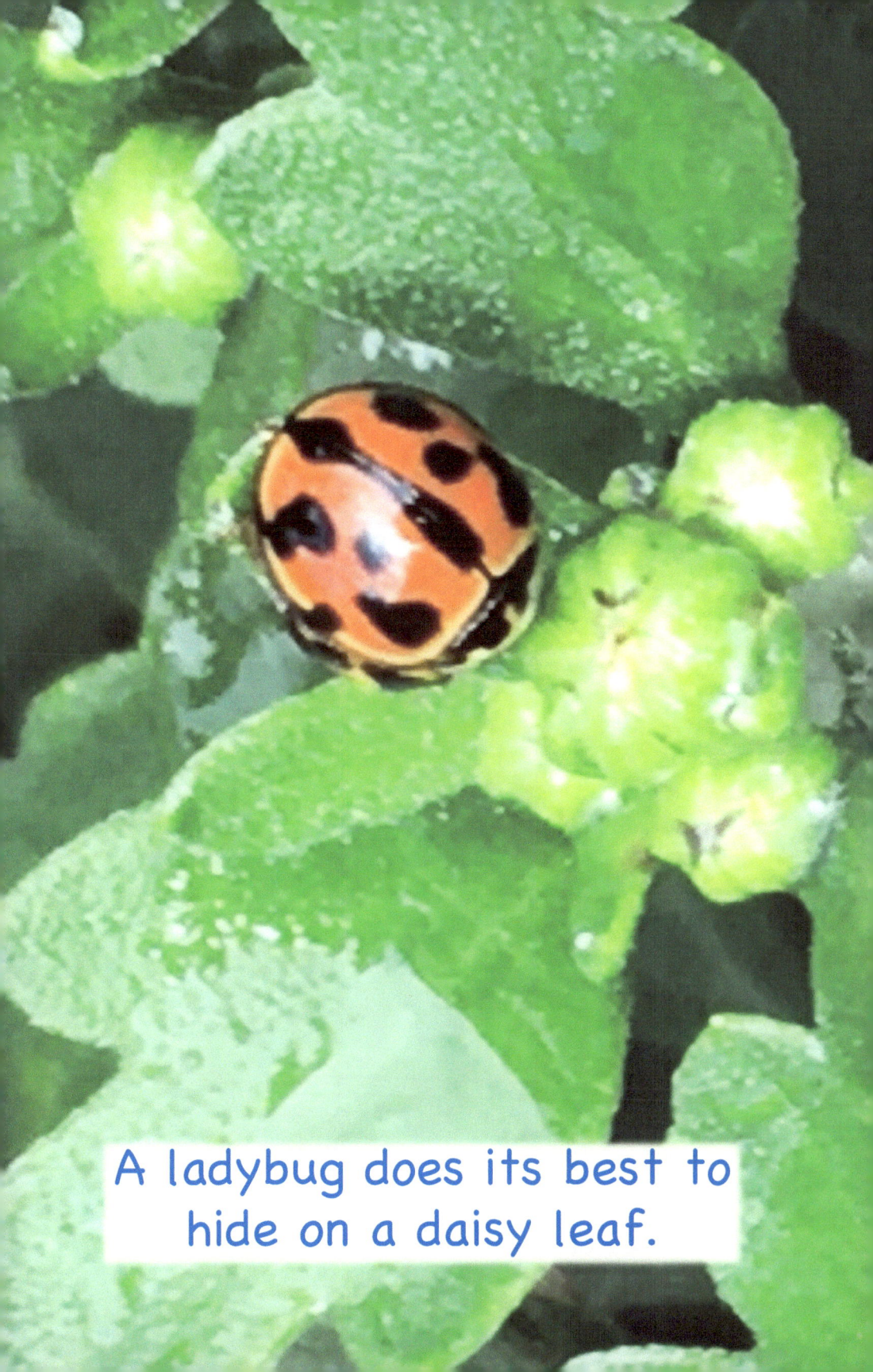

A ladybug does its best to hide on a daisy leaf.

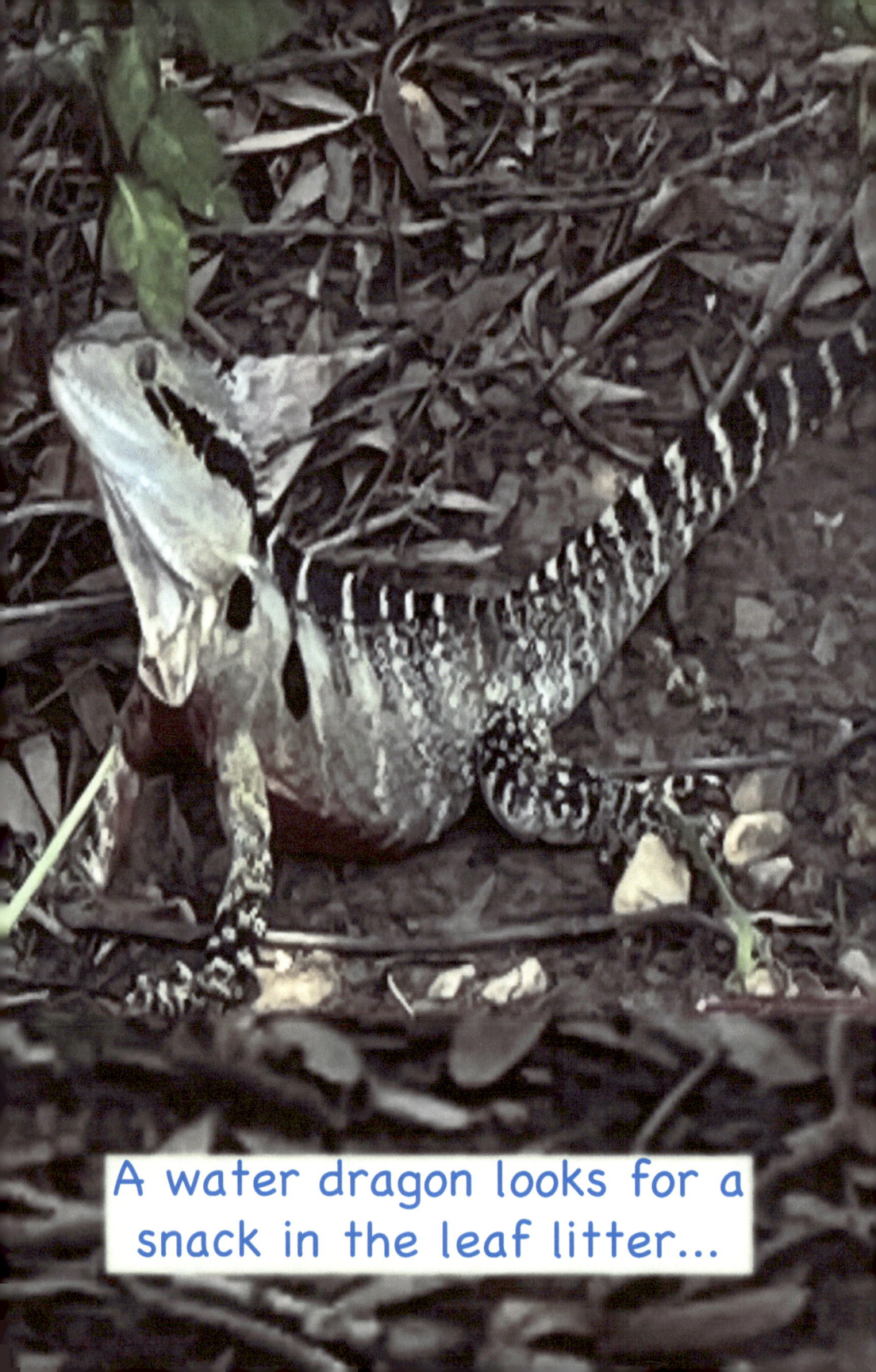

A water dragon looks for a snack in the leaf litter...

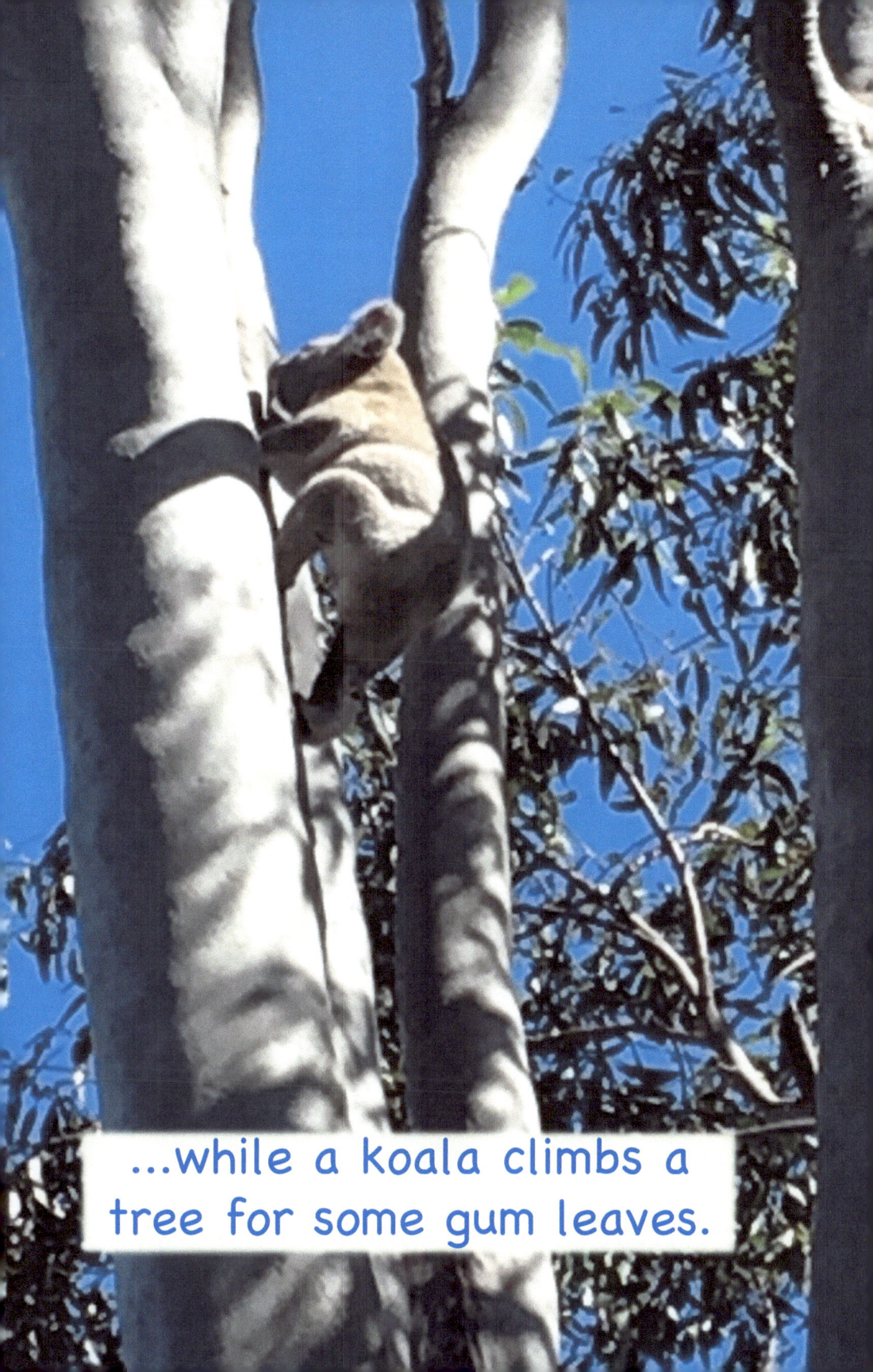

...while a koala climbs a tree for some gum leaves.

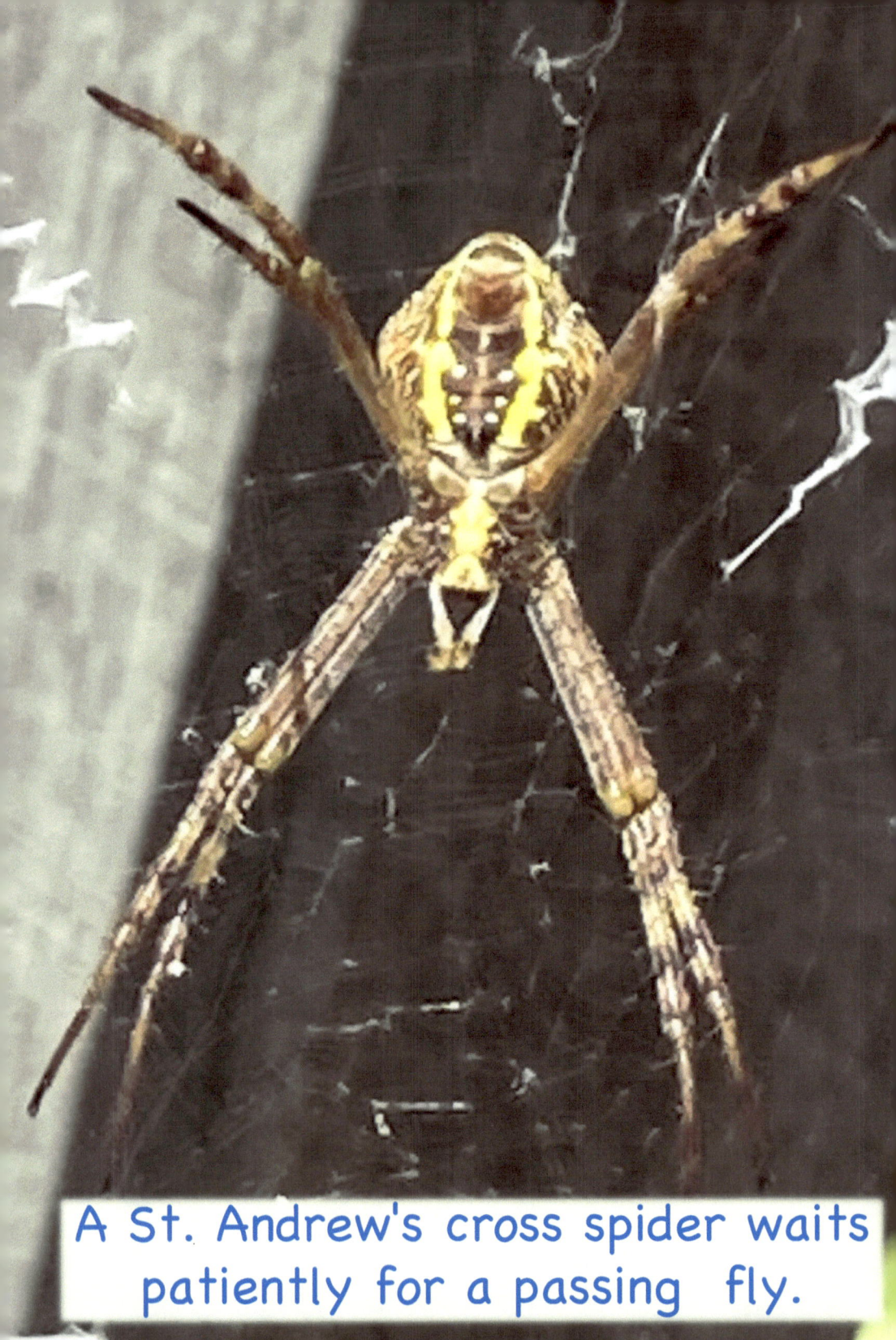

A St. Andrew's cross spider waits patiently for a passing fly.

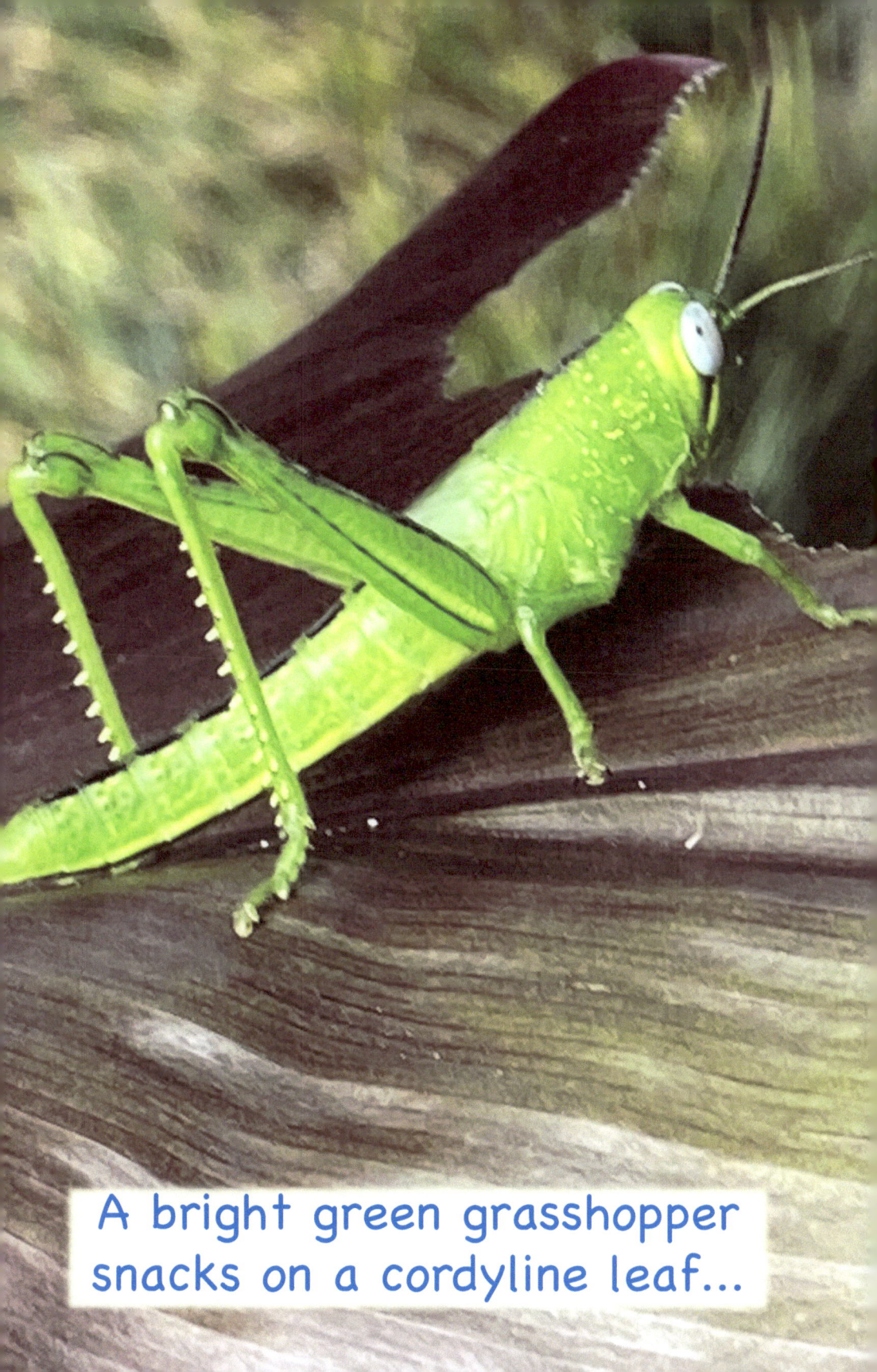

A bright green grasshopper snacks on a cordyline leaf...

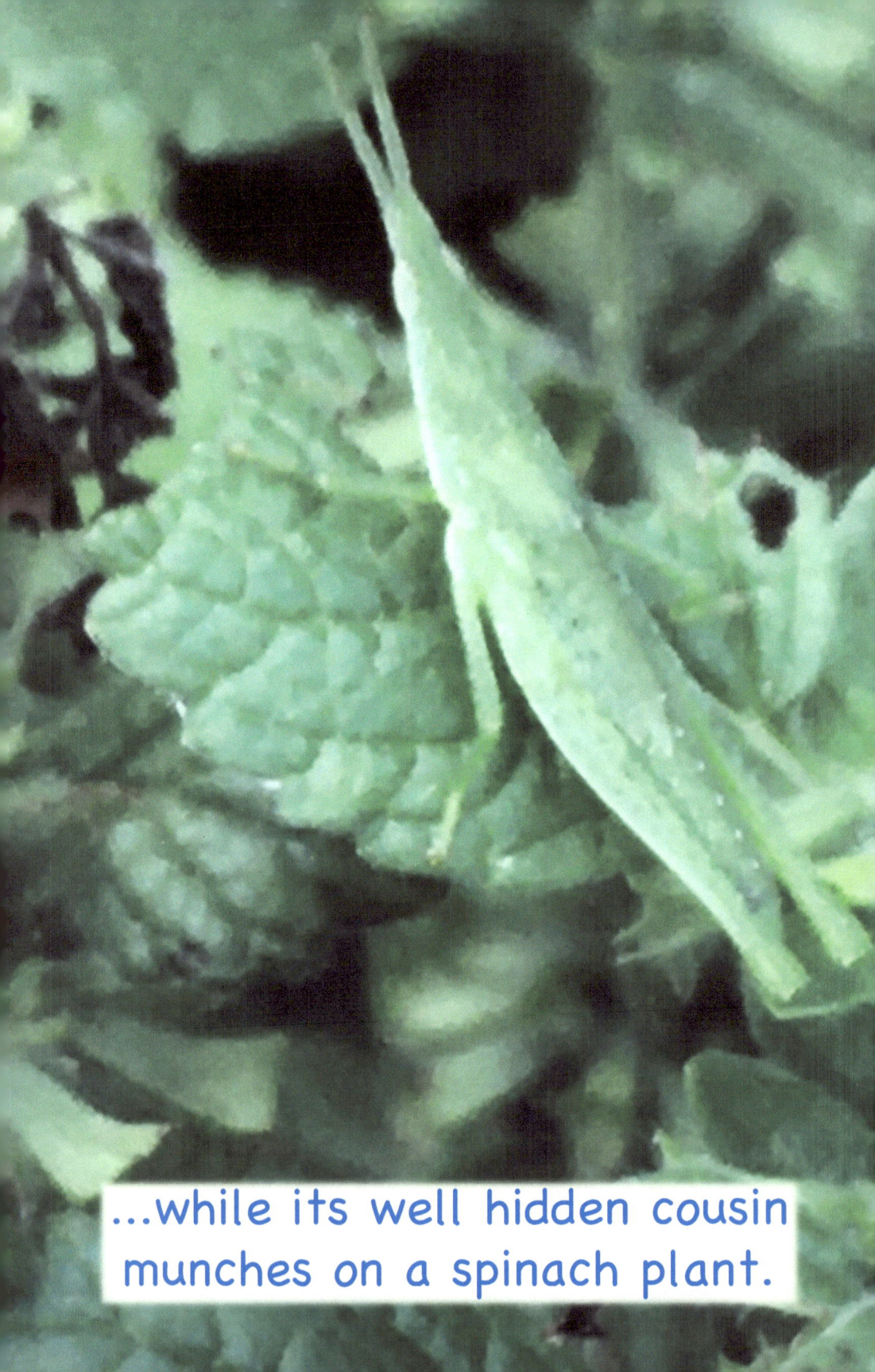

...while its well hidden cousin munches on a spinach plant.

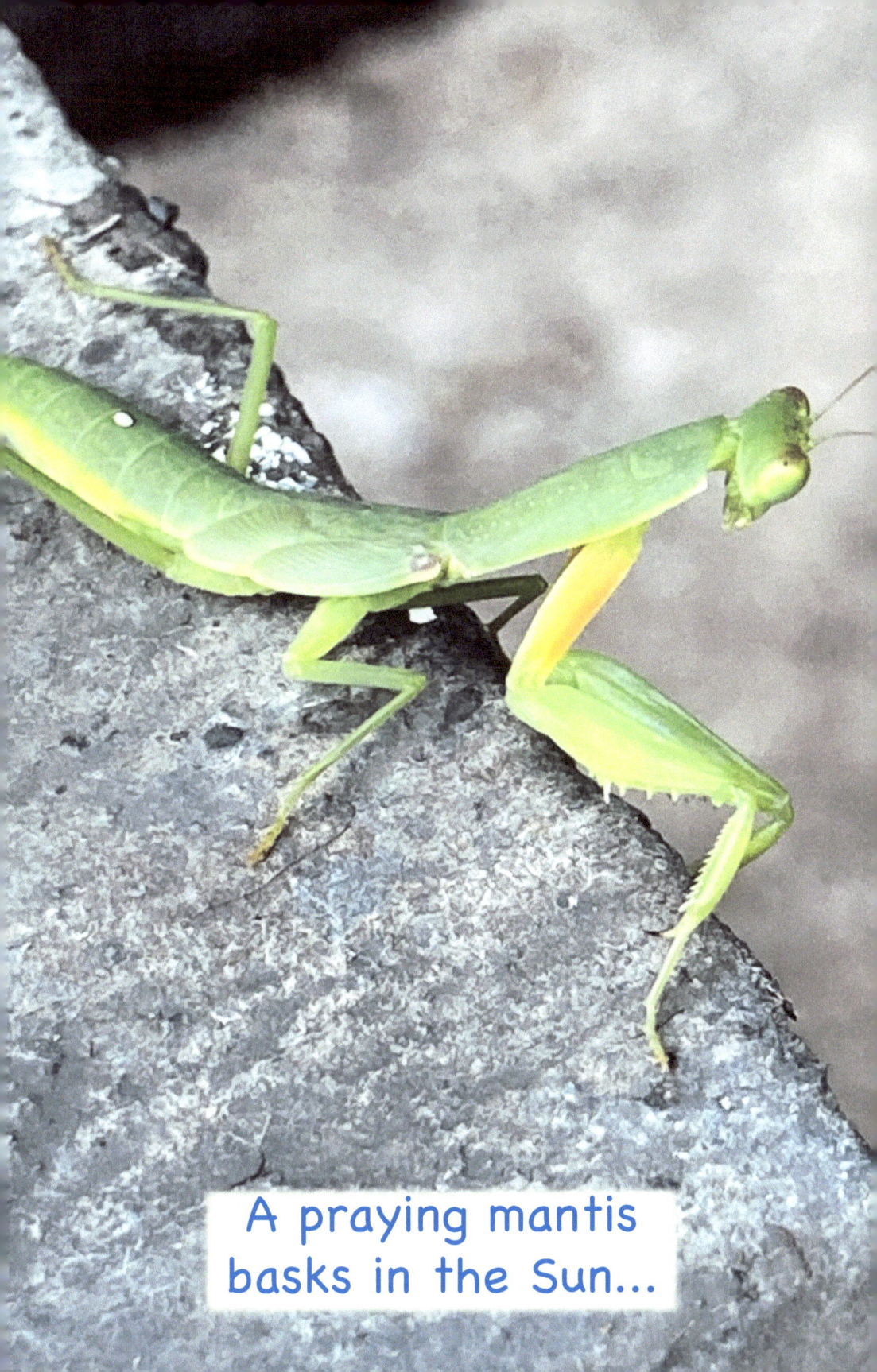

A praying mantis
basks in the Sun...

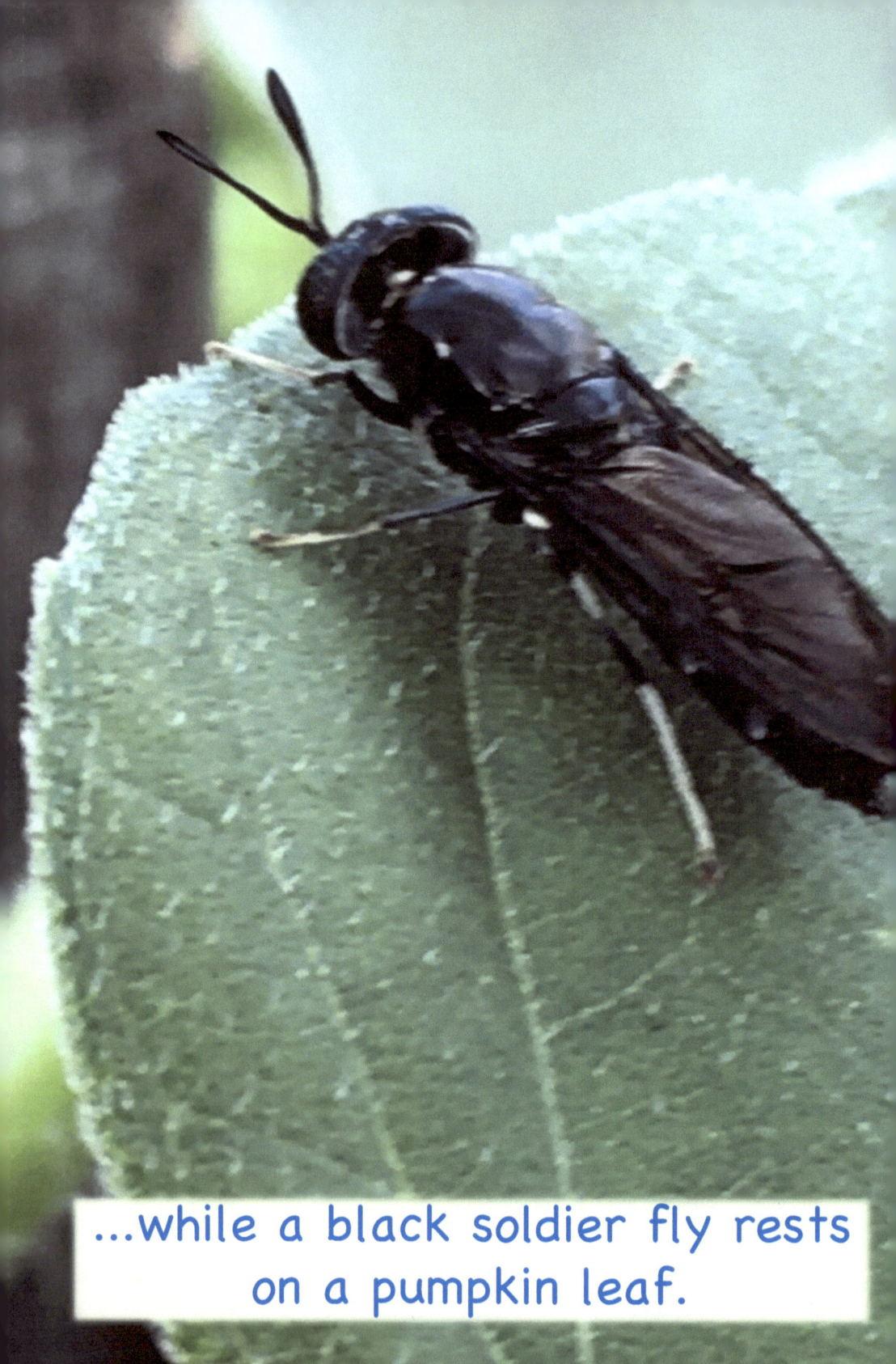

...while a black soldier fly rests on a pumpkin leaf.

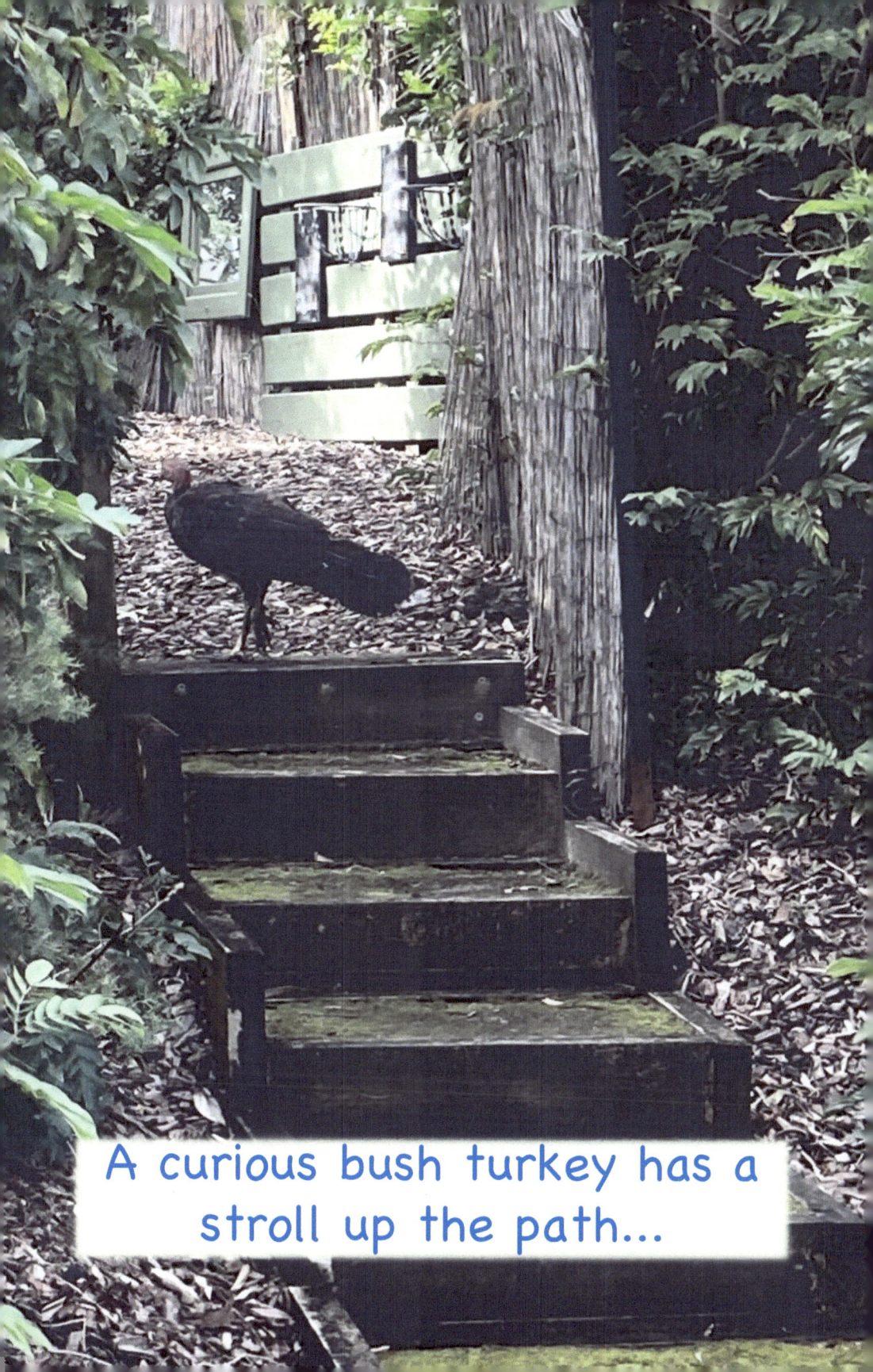

A curious bush turkey has a stroll up the path...

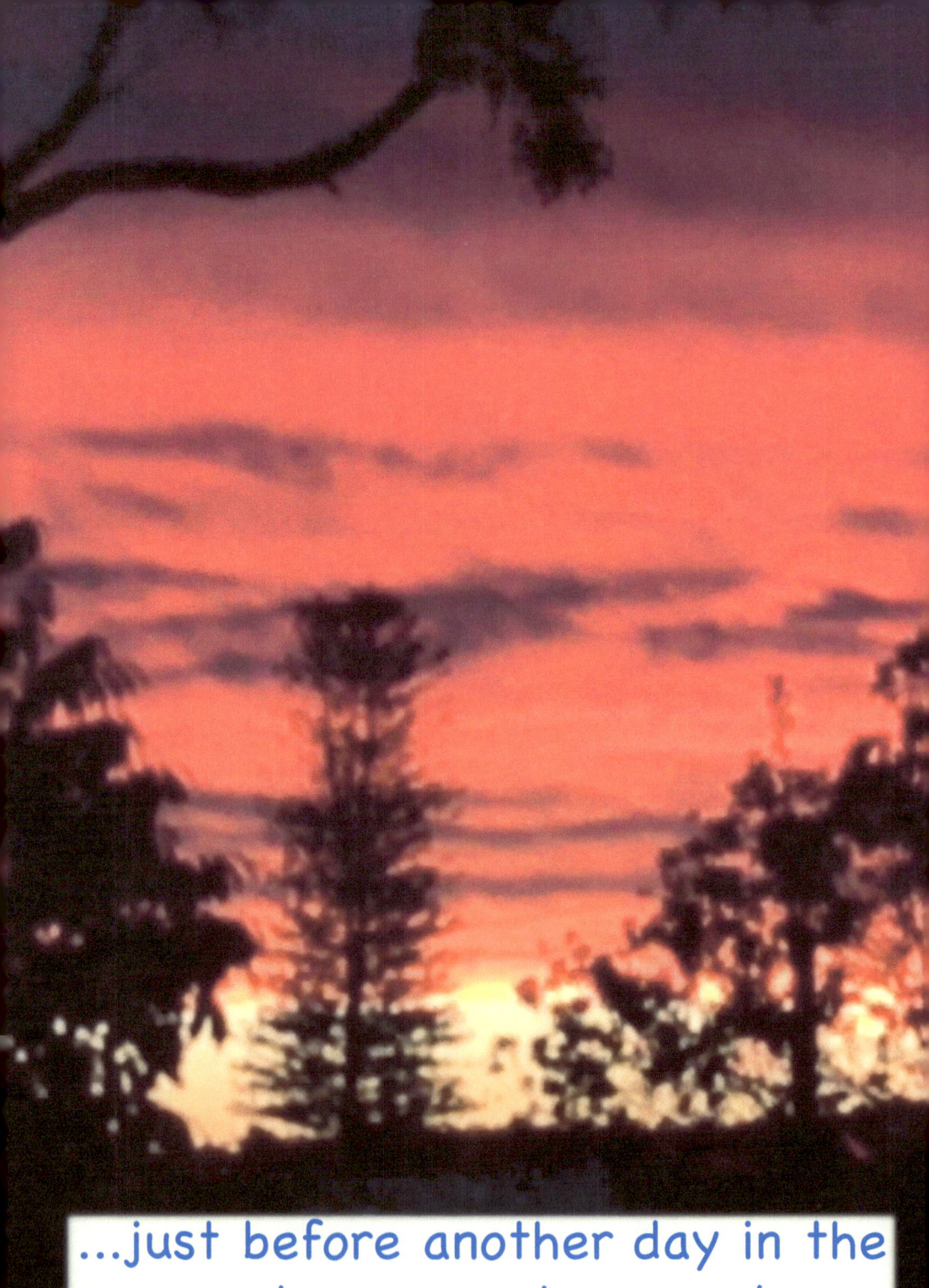

...just before another day in the garden comes to an end.

www.ingramcontent.com/pod-product-compliance
Lightning Source LLC
Chambersburg PA
CBHW050843290526
45792CB00002B/507